Education for Mission

J. Allan Ranck

EDUCATION

for

MISSION

friendship press   new york

To my mother and father

devoted Christians
whose farm home had world horizons

ACKNOWLEDGMENTS

Education for Mission inherits much from a book that has been a vital source of information and inspiration in thousands of churches in North America. That book is *Missionary Education in Your Church,* by Nevin C. Harner and David D. Baker.

The author has many obligations to the members of the Board of Managers of the Commission on Missionary Education, the National Council of the Churches of Christ in the U.S.A. His association with them, first as a fellow denominational leader in missionary education and in recent years as a member of their staff, has made it possible to draw together such insights and suggestions as are contained in this book. In a real way, the book is the product of the joint efforts of all those who have responsibility for missionary education in the denominations of Canada and the United States. The author has relied heavily on their manuals, curriculum materials, and interpretative literature.

Grateful thanks are given to the author's fellow staff members. Frequent and stimulating conversations with them are reflected throughout *Education for Mission*.

The editors of the book have been creative and encouraging partners in the developing of it. Special gratitude is expressed to Miss Edna Green for typing the manuscript. Several other members of the staff of the Commission carried extra responsibilities to allow the writer additional time for the book.

Finally, the author records his appreciation to his wife and his daughters, who supplied encouragement and inspiration when they were needed.

Contents

Contents

I

The Mission, the Church, and the Christian

THE CHURCH BELONGS TO JESUS CHRIST. THIS affirmation is the basis for education for mission, the learning and growing experience by which Christians become involved in the mission of the church.

The church is the fellowship in faith of persons called together by their Lord, Jesus Christ. They worship God as they know him through Christ. Guided by the Holy Spirit, they study Scripture, pray, and participate in the life and work of Christ in the world. The church acknowledges its Lord through use of Word and sacrament, makes him known to others, and receives into fellowship those who respond in faith to him.

Christ's church lives in all times and in all places. Pentecost was its birthday; from that time the disciples scattered into the world in the spirit of their risen and living Lord to carry on his mission. In each following generation, the church has witnessed to the world in the name of its divine Leader.

The church today is divided into denominations based on particular beliefs, traditions, and forms of government. There are three general classifications of Christian churches —Protestant, Eastern Orthodox, and Roman Catholic—and a variety of denominations, national churches, or orders exist within them.

Despite these differences, a mysterious and majestic oneness abides in the church. The one Lord of the church gives his church unity. The Apostle Paul wrote of one body, one Spirit, one hope, one Lord, one faith, one baptism, one God and Father of all. Today, through the ecumenical movement, Protestant and Orthodox Christians seek to rediscover the meaning of that unity—the oneness of Christ's church in the whole world and in all times. A local congregation, the one we call "our church," is encircled in this oneness. It is a congregation of Christians in denominational and interdenominational fellowship with other congregations; but beyond this, it shares in the nature and life of the one, holy body of Christ.

In this profile of the church there are many characteristics of mission. It is clear that we cannot inform ourselves about the church without becoming informed about mission.

THE MISSIONARY NATURE OF THE CHURCH

The ecumenical movement symbolizes not only a keener awareness of the church's unity but a fresh understanding of the oneness of the church in mission. We see that, because it has one Lord, the church is one. It thereby has one mission, one purpose for its existence. That mission is to make Jesus Christ known to the world and to accomplish the mission that Jesus himself came to achieve. Jesus knew that he had been sent into the world to do the work of God, his Father. His life and death were devoted to it, and his resurrection declared the vindication and victory of it all.

To his disciples and his church, Christ said, "As the Father has sent me, even so I send you." (John 20:21.) He sends his church into the world to make God known, as God made himself known in Jesus Christ. God's purpose is to redeem men so that they may live as his children, in fulfillment of the destiny for which he created them. In Paul's words: ". . . God was in Christ reconciling the world to himself, not counting their trespasses against them and entrusting to us the message of reconciliation." (II Cor. 5:19.)

What we call "our church" belongs to Christ and we belong to him and to it. Our church exists only for the purpose of Christ's mission.

A local church fulfills its mission in part in its own community. Its services are familiar to all of us. It brings people into its fellowship. It teaches. It speaks and acts on community issues. It offers Christian fellowship. It leads people into God's presence through Word and sacrament in the worshiping community. Worship, education, evangelism, service, and fellowship characterize the activities of a Christian church.

When Christians help extend these ministries to other

communities close at hand or on the farthest horizons, they
are affirming the New Testament's teaching that the mission is to reach from "Jerusalem and Judea" to "Samaria
and to the end of the earth." We have come to identify
this reaching out as the missionary work of the church.
Christian missions exist to tell the good news of the gospel.
Their aim is to establish the church in every place, working
in partnership with people who confess Jesus Christ as their
Savior and Lord. The men and women who do this missions
work are called missionaries. Their activities include education, evangelism, worship, service, and fellowship, the same
activities that characterize a faithful church anywhere.

This concept of *missions* to other lands and peoples must
not lead us to think that *mission* consists solely in reaching
out to communities beyond our own. We must comprehend
that we are involved in mission as much in the spot where
we live as is anyone at any other place on earth.

The mission of the church is like a pool of water into
which thousands of pebbles are dropped. Concentric circles move out from the place where each pebble breaks the
surface, and the circles mingle with one another until the
whole pool is agitated. There is not just one center from
which the circles expand; there are centers everywhere. The
mission is like a network of broadcasting stations whose
messages radiate to the whole world, making possible inter-
communication. Wherever there is a church, or for that
matter, an individual Christian, the mission begins. From
the center it moves out until it involves the church and the
Christian in the evangelization of the whole world.

THE DUTY OF EVERY CHRISTIAN

From the human point of view, a church is its members, singly and corporately. Therefore, every Christian as a part of the church shares in its mission. His influence may be positive or negative, but he cannot divest himself of the mission. It is not an elective course, a special interest for a few. If a man is a Christian, if he belongs to a church, he bears responsibility for the church's mission.

In fact, every Christian is a missionary. Other people may still represent him in those places where he himself cannot be present. But where he is, he too plays a role in the total mission of the church. His attitude and actions will either advance the cause of Christ or they will hinder it. If he is a hinderer in his own community, it will do little good for him to share in supporting men and women who are missionaries in the professional sense. What is gained for the church at one place will be lost at the other.

This missionary responsibility affects the daily life of every Christian who comprehends his work as a holy vocation. It is expressed in such ways as industry and integrity. Paul wrote of Prisca and Aquila, who "risked their necks for my life," of Andronicus and Junias as "men of note among the apostles," of Mary, who "has worked hard among you." We may assume that their new faith showed itself clearly to the communities in which they lived. In our society, for all its evils, many persons recognize their daily work as a holy vocation. A lumberman in the state of Washington, for example, conducts his business as a trust from

God and channels a large share of his profits into Christian missions.

Involvement in mission compels us to participate in the community's social and civic affairs. We act in mission when we vote, and when we volunteer to work for the Community Chest. Parent-teacher associations, school boards, town governments, social clubs—they are all avenues for Christian witness and service. The will of God will be done in the critical circles of human relationship only as Christian men and women spend themselves unselfishly to serve their communities.

Year by year, increasing numbers of people, many of them church members, travel from their homelands to places they have never before visited. Some are business and government representatives who take up residence in other lands on tours of duty. These persons have many of the opportunities for witness and service open to professional missionaries. Their situations are extremely important; they live and work among people of other faiths and cultures who are likely to judge their religion by their actions.

Our participation in mission involves our attitudes, opinions, and convictions. In these times of controversial social issues and international tension, what Christian people think and how they express their thoughts are important. Attitudes of love, forgiveness, generosity, compassion, peace, and world-mindedness support Christian mission. Bigotry, prejudice, pride, indifference, and supernationalism undermine it.

When a person is so committed to mission that its influence shapes all the associations of his life—his business or profession, his civic activities, his attitudes, for example— he cannot help but be an ardent and intelligent supporter of those missions that are seeking to extend the blessings of Christ's kingdom everywhere in the world. He will have vigorous appreciation of the need for giving personnel, money, and skills to strengthen Christian missions in any part of the earth where those resources are needed.

EDUCATION FOR MISSION

We have been describing in simple terms something of the breadth and depth of Christianity today. It is important that we comprehend these dimensions, for they measure our objectives in education for mission. With them as reference, we can identify specifically some of the goals toward which we reach.

Education for mission seeks to develop the involvement of every Christian in the church's mission. It answers questions about the validity of missionary activity by leading to deeper understanding of the gospel and thorough knowledge of missionary work. It dispels indifference through information and involvement, and it inspires support of missionary work.

When we undertake education for mission in our church, we come in contact with the achievements and problems of the world-wide Christian mission. The church door opens on distant horizons, and we meet the people of Asia, of Africa, of South America, and of the unfamiliar communities in our own land. We learn of the progress of these our brothers toward fuller freedom and abundance; of their needs; of the full ministries of the Christian church to be extended to them.

Education for mission moves us to pray—one thing that all Christians everywhere can do for others. We pray for the health of the church and for the people to whom the gospel of Christ brings its good news. In this resource, we are completely unlimited, for the powers we summon are the infinite activities of the Holy Spirit. We pray in hope and trust. We are led to pray with understanding and faith, and to live as we pray in Christian obedience.

The sharing of money, skill, and time to support the Christian mission at home and around the world will grow naturally out of education for mission. This stewardship is based on our understanding that everything that we are and have ultimately belongs to God. When this idea impels us, we distribute our resources in ways that will witness to Christ effectively, wherever that help is needed and desired. So long as Canadians and Americans, constituting only about 6 per cent of the world's population, can claim almost 50 per cent of the world's annual income, they have a special responsibility to give generously for the growth of the Christian church.

Education for mission opens doors for many young people. Exploring the gospel and discovering its meaning for the whole world will lead some young men and women to offer themselves to the church so that they might venture into new frontiers of mission. Denominations, however, exercise extreme care in matching candidate with position.

Missionaries or fraternal workers must be the best representatives the church can find, animated by the highest motives, equipped with the best skills, disposed to work in mission with—not simply to—the people they have come to help. Young people need patient and wise counseling to face possible disappointment, delay, and difficulty until at last each one may find some useful place in the missionary effort. Stringent health requirements sometimes prevent a young person from receiving an appointment when all other conditions have been met. Sometimes an appointment is delayed because there are no openings requiring the precise set of qualifications of the candidate.

Many of our churches' young people may find opportunity for service and witness overseas in work with government programs, businesses or industries, or service agencies. Their witness will be most effective if they combine trained minds with the spirit of Christian service. One example is that of a young engineer with General Electric Corporation who frequently travels to South American countries. He does his job competently; he admires and respects the South Americans with whom he works. His associations have benefited him both personally and professionally. He worships with Latin American friends in their churches when he can and identifies himself as much as possible with their problems and hopes.

Opportunities for a missionary vocation, official or unofficial, are open to middle-aged or retired business or professional people, also. These people may render valuable short-term service, finding in it a new joy and the fulfillment of an already useful life of service. A doctor, on leave of absence from his own duties, supervised a hospital in Nigeria while the regular missionary doctor took his much-needed furlough. A builder spent several years after retirement assisting with a construction program in Burma. A retired professional church worker became a housemother for an educational institution.

AND OUR CHURCH?

All of us might be able to cite other evidence to show that education for mission transforms the lives of people and of churches. At the same time, we would have to confess that such transformations don't occur often enough. When we ask why, we turn the spotlight of inquiry on the churches of which we are a part.

When each of us examines his own congregation, can we say that it is aware of its mission? Is it a missionary church? Does it apply itself to witness in its own community with the same imagination and devotion that it would expect of missionaries sent to other fields? Does it show as much interest in the growth of the church elsewhere as it does in its own growth?

Wherever such inquiry reveals that commitment to mission is weak or absent, every member of the congregation bears the responsibility for its growth. The task is not the minister's alone, though he should play a significant role. Each church member is equally responsible, simply because of his relationship to God who has called him to witness and service.

2

The Mission in God's Plan

MEN AND WOMEN WHO ARE COMMITTED TO the Christian mission and who try to lead others to a similar commitment inevitably meet resistance from some people. The arguments are familiar: Education for mission is a technique of church leaders to stir up support for missions; it's just a dream of some Christian enthusiasts trying to make the church effective in an unchristian world.

The only way to respond to such attitudes is to share our conviction that the Christian mission is based on confidence in God's redeeming activity in the world through the church. The call to mission is the word of God to the Christian, spoken through the Bible and the Holy Spirit.

One of the most familiar missionary commands of Holy Scripture are Jesus' words to the disciples before his ascension, ". . . you shall be my witnesses in Jerusalem and in all Judea and Samaria and to the end of the earth." (Acts 1:8.) Another is the passage known as the Great Commis-

sion, "Go therefore and make disciples of all nations, bap-
tizing them in the name of the Father and of the Son and
of the Holy Spirit, teaching them to observe all that I have
commanded you; and lo, I am with you always, to the close
of the age." (Matt. 28:19-20.)

These two commands make vivid and clear the fact of
our mission and how the early church understood it. They
leave no doubt as to how the risen Christ expected his gospel to be made known.

GOD'S REDEEMING ACTIVITY

The missionary calling of the church rests not only on
certain commands but on Jesus Christ himself. God made
himself fully known to us in Jesus Christ after centuries of
reaching out to man through other means. He showed his
love for men in Jesus' birth, in his life, and above all in his
death and resurrection. And it was Jesus who sent his disciples into the world to witness to the redeeming purpose
and activity of God among men.

Charles Ranson gets at the heart of it in his book, *That
the World May Know.* "If we are asked 'By what authority?' we can only answer—in the last analysis—'In the name
of Jesus.'

" 'As the Father has sent me, even so send I you,' said the
risen Christ to his earliest disciples. These words, which
are the charter of the unchanging mission of the church,
presuppose the whole majestic purpose of God in creation
and in human history. They likewise define the nature of
the church as a missionary community—a fellowship of

those who in every age are sent to make known to the world God's purpose of creative love, the mighty acts by which men's deliverance has been wrought, and the continuing design by which a new humanity is to be brought to birth."[1]

God's redeeming activity, the source of Christian mission, is apparent throughout the Old Testament. He created the universe and everything in it, and he loved his creation. When men alienated themselves from him, he forgave and redeemed them in his love. He chastised and instructed them so that they might know him and live in fellowship with him. Ultimately, he called Israel to be his chosen and holy people, that they might be his witness to the nations.

If in many ways it seems that the Old Testament is only the account of God's particular interest in Israel, we should remember that it was through this chosen people that he brought his Son to the world. From the life, death, and resurrection of that Son, the Savior of the world, springs the new people of God, who now are his witnesses to the nations.

Stephen Neill, in *The Unfinished Task*, describes the relationship of Israel to the Christian mission: "The purpose of God which was fulfilled in the history of Israel was twofold; first, the provision of a homeland, within which Christ the Son of God could be born and grow and accomplish His work; and secondly, the preparation through the Diaspora of a wider world in which the Gospel could quickly take

[1] Ranson, Charles W. *That the World May Know*. New York: Friendship Press, 1953, p. 47.

root, and in which the Church would quickly develop to such maturity as would enable it to survive the destruction of the Jewish nation and the collapse of the Roman Empire."[2]

Jesus' contemporaries and countrymen were brought up in the heritage of Israel. Some of them came to recognize him as the Savior and Lord for whom their forefathers had longed, God's Word of hope and salvation to the world. They were transformed by their relationship with him and gave themselves in discipleship to his mission.

The New Testament records God's redeeming love and reconciling act in Jesus Christ and makes the Christian mission explicitly known. The missionary motive is most obvious in the Book of the Acts of the Apostles, the exciting history of the deeds of Christ's first witnesses. It is clearly seen in Paul's letters as he describes his own missionary adventures and charges the young churches to take up the mission. It is implicit in the Gospels, the immortal accounts of the life, death, and resurrection of the Lord of the mission.

To understand the Christian mission, Bishop Lesslie Newbigin says, "We have to begin from the New Testament. The Church's mission is none other than the carrying out of the mission of Christ Himself. 'As the Father has sent me even so send I you.' How shall we define that mission? It would be a mistake to attempt to sum it up in a simple formula, when the New Testament itself contains such a

[2] Neill, Stephen. *The Unfinished Task.* London, Eng.: Lutterworth Press, 1957, p. 29.

wide variety of language on the subject. We might begin with our Lord's own account of it: 'The Spirit of the Lord is upon me, because he has anointed me to preach good news to the poor. He has sent me to proclaim release to the captives, and recovering of sight to the blind, to set at liberty those who are oppressed, to proclaim the acceptable year of the Lord.' The record in the four gospels shows us how the programme was carried out. The various apostolic writers give us their summaries and interpretations of it. He was sent to do God's will. He came to make the Father's Name known. He came to manifest and establish the righteousness of God. He came that men might believe, and be justified. He came that they might have peace with God. He came to reconcile the world to God. He came that men might have life. He came to seek and save the lost. He came not to be served but to serve and to give His life as ransom for many. All these phrases represent only a small selection of the relevant language of the New Testament. . . ."[3]

The first century Christians were witnesses of these activities as their Lord had urged them to be. They told of their new life in Christ. Paul wrote what many must have felt, even when their Christian testimony meant suffering or death: "For necessity is laid upon me. Woe to me if I do not preach the gospel . . . I am entrusted with a commission." (I Cor. 9:16-17.)

[3] Newbigin, Lesslie. *One Body, One Gospel, One World; The Christian Mission Today.* London, Eng.: International Missionary Council, 1958, pp. 17-18.

CHRIST'S BODY—THE CHURCH

The gospel was preached, and somehow, out of the lives of men and women living in humble situations and scattered communities, the church came into being. It exists today, vastly changed in outward appearance from those first tiny congregations, and yet irrevocably the same in essence and purpose. Its work is the work of Jesus Christ— to preach good tidings to the poor, to proclaim release to the captives, to restore the sight of the blind, to set at liberty them that are bruised, to proclaim the acceptable year of the Lord.

Every church member, no matter what he feels about the Christian mission, would agree that the church should strive to make God's redeeming love known in the service of men's needs, in the fulfilling of their lives, in lifting them to their full stature as sons of God. This is more than humanitarian service; it involves discovering the profoundest needs of men and then bringing to those needs the remedy that can fully meet them.

The church in its missionary outreach has always engaged in this sort of service. We need only to observe a mission hospital or clinic for a day or so to feel overwhelmed by the privilege of bringing to hundreds of people the prospect of renewed health, relief from pain, and deliverance from crippling disease. The light in the face of the new literate who excitedly shouts, "I can read," underscores the value of literacy programs, while the extensive development of educational institutions contributes an ever-growing number of Christian-trained leaders. Such deeds, done in the name and spirit of Christ, witness to his love.

The essential quality of the mission is love, and those who engage in mission must be drawn together by the love they proclaim to the world. This has not always been true of Christian groups. There have been periods when the church—the body of Christ—has been broken by enmity, selfishness, intolerance, and bigotry. Paul warned the early church against such separations. "Is Christ divided?" he asked. "I appeal to you, brethren, by the name of our Lord Jesus Christ, that all of you agree that there be no dissensions among you, but that you be united in the same mind and the same judgment." (I Cor. 1:10.) Jesus established the criterion for discipleship when he said, "By this all men will know that you are my disciples, if you have love for one another." (John 13:35.)

In recent years, Christian fellowship and understanding have been increasing through the ecumenical movement. Christian missions have been the primary stimulus in this movement. As missionaries and other church leaders have worked together and have gathered in world conferences to consider their mission, they have sensed the Spirit of God drawing them together. Many Christians are now seeking to heal the divisions in the church and to express more fully the unifying love of its one Lord.

Numerous developments toward Christian unity have occurred on mission fields. Union seminaries have trained ministers for various denominations. Hospitals and secondary schools have been united. Church unions, such as the Church of South India, the United Church of Christ in the Philippines, the United Church of Canada, and the Church of Christ in Thailand, have been consummated. Where Christians are a small minority in the population, co-operation and unity become a vital necessity. How indeed can the gigantic task of winning our own continent for Christ be accomplished apart from the co-operation of all Christians, drawn together in their one Lord? As Christ prayed, "that they may all be one . . . that the world may believe . . ." so also should his church pray.

THE CHURCH AND THE WORLD

The same love that binds the church together as a body also binds the church to the world. "For God so loved the world that he gave his only Son, that whoever believes in him should not perish but have eternal life. For God sent the Son into the world, not to condemn the world, but that the world might be saved through him." (John 3:16-17.) The Christian church must love the world unselfishly if it is to accomplish its redemptive mission among men. Such love does not mean conformity to the world. Transformed in the spirit of Jesus Christ, Christians love the world and its people by giving themselves in service of truth and justice. Jesus prayed for the church, "I do not pray that thou shouldst take them out of the world, but that thou shouldst keep them from the evil one. They are not of the world, even as I am not of the world. Sanctify them in the truth; thy word is truth. As thou didst send me into the world, so I have sent them into the world. And for their sake I consecrate myself, that they also may be consecrated in truth." (John 17:15-19.)

There is always a risk to the church as it seeks to live in mission in the midst of the world. If the church speaks out on unjust practices in government, business, or union management, critics will blame it for meddling in private matters. When it involves itself in social issues, it incurs the wrath of those whose wrongs it condemns. Living in the world, it may become like the world. Churches in non-Christian cultures are confronted by a dilemma: how much to withdraw from society, and yet how to be identified with society enough to play a vital role in the lives of the people. The greater risk for the church is in isolating itself so completely from society that it becomes irrelevant and powerless. When the church, like its Lord, gives itself in sacrificial, redemptive love to the world, it has the power to transform and recreate.

GOOD NEWS TO TELL

New Testament study throws light on some of the particulars of the Christian mission. Take the fact that the gospel is good news, and that, possessing it, we must share it with others. Peter and John told their accusers and persecutors, ". . . we cannot but speak of what we have seen and heard." (Acts 4:20.) And it was said of them later that ". . . every day in the temple and at home they did not cease teaching and preaching Jesus as the Christ." (Acts 5:42.) The excitement and conviction of the encounter with Jesus Christ sends a true disciple out to tell others about the experience. When the gospel is perceived as good news, it cannot be kept back.

The Christian mission suffers in many places today because this sense of good news seems lost. Being a Christian has become acceptable and popular. The radical nature of the new life in Christ is obscured. A missionary in Hong Kong observed that third and fourth generation Christians in Taiwan seem to lose much of the exhilaration that characterized the earlier converts to the Christian faith. In Korea, where some years ago every new convert was expected to bring another to Jesus Christ before he himself was accepted in the fellowship of the church, the same tendency has appeared as the church matured. As churches grow more highly institutionalized, they tend to lose the fire of their evangelistic fervor and the joy of their spiritual inheritance. Christians must seek for constantly fresh joy in the experience of salvation if the mission is to be effective through them. They must retain the surprise that the good news of the gospel creates in men when they first hear it.

RECONCILING LOVE

The good news itself is most important: God loves every person and desires his redemption. He sent his Son to earth in human form so that men could know how closely God indentifies himself with their needs. In Christ, God served men in love, bore their sufferings, died for them, and rose in victory over every mortal fear. When this love was comprehended by early Christians, they put it in such words as Paul's: "God was in Christ reconciling the world to himself." (II Cor. 5:19.) In our world of estrangement and loneliness, the reconciliation of men with God and of men with each other becomes great good news. This is something to make known to persons; it is something to heal the breaches between nations. It is a mission that deserves the loyal involvement of every Christian.

Not only do we know that God is seeking to reconcile men to himself and to one another, but we know, too, that Christians are to be ambassadors of reconciliation. One of the most rewarding personal experiences is to be a messenger of hope, a healer of wounds, a mediator between persons.

At the Third World Conference of Christian Youth, in Travancore, India, about seven years after the close of the second world war, an early morning prayer service was held. Young people from Japan and young people from the Philippines met in the presence of their common Lord. Animosity and reserve melted as they prayed together for forgiveness and for fellowship. Only a little later, a similar meeting between Dutch and Indonesian young people was held. Reconciliation was accomplished by the work of the Spirit of Christ. In the United States, when tension has been high between white and Negro groups, some Christians have contributed to creative reconciliation through interracial occasions of prayer, study, and fellowship.

The danger always looms large that the spirit of love and reconciliation may not be expressed with enough daring and courage. Unhealed wounds fester and grow worse.

Speaking of the failure of whites in South Africa to be reconciled with their black countrymen, Alan Paton in *Cry, the Beloved Country* puts these poignant words on the lips of a young African priest: ". . . I have one great fear in my heart, that one day when they turn to loving they will find we are turned to hating."[4] The reconciling love of Christians dare not delay its mission.

THE LORD'S MISSION

The Christian discovers from the New Testament that the mission to which he is called is not really *his* mission; it is the mission of his Lord. Paul denied any personal status in his calling by declaring: "For what we preach is not ourselves, but Jesus Christ as Lord, with ourselves as your servants for Jesus' sake. For it is the God who said, 'Let light shine out of darkness,' who has shone in our hearts to give the light of the knowledge of the glory of God in the face of Christ." (II Cor. 4:5-6.)

The future of the Christian mission does not depend on our cleverness, our power, or our goodness. We are only required to be faithful witnesses. We must not be presumptuous, yet there is a holy audacity in Christianity that convinces us that it is necessary for all men. Our boast is in Jesus Christ. We, his followers, are humbly convinced that he is the way, the truth, and the life. In that honest conviction, we seek to comprehend our mission and to perform it where we live and in the whole world.

[4] Paton, Alan. *Cry, the Beloved Country; A Story of Comfort in Desolation.* New York: Charles Scribner's Sons, 1948, p. 272.

3

The Mission Today

NINETEEN HUNDRED YEARS AGO, CHRISTIANS were a tiny minority living for the most part on the fringes of a European empire. "Today," in the words of William Richey Hogg, "with three or four minor exceptions, the Christian church is found in every land around the world."[1]

Such growth might make it seem that the work of Christian missions has been accomplished and that, consequently, education for mission is no longer necessary in the life of the church. No interpretation of facts could be more in error, and none prove more certainly that education, instead of being abandoned, requires the fullest investment of time and energy.

We live in a new day in Christian mission, a time of massive uncertainties, complex concerns, unrealized resources. Only as the uncertainties are cleared, the com-

[1] Hogg, William Richey. *One World, One Mission*. New York: Friendship Press, 1960, p. 47.

plexities resolved, and the resources tapped, shall we be able to fulfill the mission with which we are entrusted. These tasks are of vital interest in education for mission.

To understand this new day, we should review quickly the days that preceded it. Their story is unbelievable, and their heroes were some of the most remarkable individuals that the world has ever known.

CHRISTIAN EXPANSION

The Christians of the first centuries after Jesus overcame persecution and prejudice with peace and love. By the fourth century, Christianity had pervaded the mighty Roman Empire and had won many of its citizens.

For the next several centuries, missionaries ventured mainly northward into the British Isles, Germany, France, and the Scandinavian countries. Heroes such as Patrick, Columba, and Columbanus risked their lives preaching Christ and establishing monasteries among the savage, warring tribes of the north countries. Christianity brought peace and order among the pagan warriors, laying the foundation for the development of the civilization of northern Europe and the British Isles.

The golden age of exploration that dawned in the fifteenth century opened new lands to the Christian gospel. Columbus, Dias, da Gama, and Magellan pushed out into the Atlantic and around the capes of Good Hope and Horn. Missionaries sailed with the explorers, planting the cross in North and South America, India, China, Japan, the Philippines, Malaya, and Indonesia. Evidence of this period of Christian expansion is seen in the Roman Catholic churches of South America, India, the Philippines, and other parts of the world.

The Eastern Orthodox churches, which refused to accept Rome's authority, carried Christianity into eastern Europe, across to China and India, and into northern Africa. The missionary zeal of these churches faltered, however, and they have not played a significant part in the world Christian mission in recent centuries.

The early Protestant churches of Europe did not immediately set out to fulfill the Lord's call to be witnesses to the ends of the earth. They were too absorbed with establishing and defending themselves, and the theology of their founders did little to fire a vigorous missionary outreach.

THE MODERN MISSIONARY MOVEMENT

In the early nineteenth century, however, Protestant churches came alive to the Christian mission. Under the inspiration of leaders like Carey, Morrison, Judson, and Moffat, they embarked on missionary enterprises that reached to the ends of the earth. Protestants in western Europe and North America established notable missionary societies that recruited large numbers of young missionaries and gathered resources to send them out. The work that these pioneers began with painful personal sacrifice has been carried on by thousands of successors.

Because of the service of such men and women, churches and church leaders have developed around the globe. Many of these churches have joined together in Christian councils in their own lands and with churches of other parts of the world in the International Missionary Council and the World Council of Churches. For the first time, there has come into being a truly world-wide fellowship of Protestant and Orthodox Christians, all increasingly sensing their responsibility in the Christian world mission.

Stephen Neill says in *The Unfinished Task:* "It seems that in recent centuries God has been calling into existence the Christian Diaspora, not now on a Mediterranean but on a world-wide scale. The net result of Christian missions, especially over the last two centuries of rapid expansion, has been exactly this—that they have brought into being the Christian Diaspora, the scattered people of God living as aliens in the midst of civilizations determined by principles other than those of the Gospel and irreconcilable with it."[2]

THE NEW DAY IN MISSION

What then about the Christian mission in this year of our Lord? Whispers are heard that the day of the missionary enterprise is over. Some people grow weary with the overwhelming task, or are confused by the new barriers. Was it worth all the effort in China? Will the work of the mission survive the turmoil in Africa? Many others have never felt the exciting impact of Christian privilege and duty that present-day circumstances generate.

[2] Neill, Stephen. *The Unfinished Task*. London, Eng.: Lutterworth Press, 1957, p. 31.

We respond to these doubters by declaring that a new day in Christian mission has broken upon us. Its signs are as bold and clear as are the headlines and television images that hammer at us daily.

We would not be true to our faith and its traditions if we did not meet the new issues of our days with courage and imagination. The Christian mission is changeless, and yet it is ever fresh and relevant. The church has responded to the alarms and challenges of every period of history with the good news of the gospel. The Apostles announced to enslaved and exploited men that the Son of God had come among them to make them free. In the Roman era, the church declared that Christian faith is a bond uniting men in fellowship, order, and good will, and a sovereignty claiming their highest allegiance. Missionaries in northern Europe brought the civilizing and fulfilling power of the gospel to barbaric tribes. In the era of exploration, the church reached out across the world to offer enlightenment and hope amid the hardships and cruelties that accompanied the conquest of lands and peoples. In the missionary movement of the last century and a half, Christians have made known the good news of the gospel wherever people have needed its message of reconciliation and love.

THE WORLD SITUATION

What kind of world do we find ourselves in today? Surely the word that best describes the situation of mankind is revolution. So far, the twentieth century has been the century of overturn and upset—for political systems, the axioms of science, and almost all the other ways by which men have tried to order their affairs. Directly or indirectly, every change has affected the mission of the church.

For example, colonialism is dying fast. The day is gone when the missionary movement can profit from the protection, encouragement, and prestige of the Western nation from which its missionaries were sent. Now, for a missionary to be a Westerner can be a handicap in Asia or Africa. People ask: Is the Christian church just another form of Western imperialism? In sincere penitence, we need to admit that we may have at times been more anxious to impress our way of life on other people than to introduce them to our eternal, universal Lord. Every missionary, indeed every Christian, must be careful not to confuse superficial expressions of culture with the essentials of the gospel. When our culture has a creative benefit to extend to others, we ought never refrain from offering it. But in the Christian mission, cultural benefits follow and come under the judgment of the gospel.

In our own nation, the mission requires that we labor to bring our whole national life under the Lordship of Christ. Harmonizing national and international policy with Christian profession is difficult. A nation's principles are severely tested in diplomacy: how can it deal justly on the one hand with traditional allies who are colonial powers and on the other with nations seeking freedom from colonialism? Policies of trade, mutual assistance, and international co-operation should embody elements of our Christian principles. When we examine such problems, we see that the Christian mission in our own homeland relates intimately to the mission of the church in the rest of the world.

We must recognize the change in relationship between peoples whose skins are of differing color. In recent history, Christendom has predominantly been identified with the white peoples. Though strong churches once existed in North Africa and in parts of Asia, they sharply declined through the centuries. Almost inevitably, the modern Christian missionary effort took on the appearance of a benevolent ministry of the white peoples to the colored peoples. Today the colored peoples, a large majority of the world's population, are coming into their own, in part because of missionary work. The new day shouts to us that the gospel is not a possession *of* the one to be shared *with* the other. The gospel is the heritage of all men, regardless of race or nation. In the mission to which it calls us, all Christians join equally before God.

Equal opportunities for minority groups in our own land are essential to the full performance of our mission. Integration in public education, unhindered franchise, fair housing, opportunities for employment without prejudice by either employers or unions, and above all full fellowship in the church are imperative.

The new day is marked by another clear sign—the turmoil of peoples all over the world. Nations are being born, and with new independence goes intense nationalism. The bright dream of sovereignty leads to stern realities. Occasionally, as with India and Pakistan, or the Congo Republic, freedom begins with civil strife and bloodshed. New na-

tions struggle for years to achieve stable economies, often
suffering severe setbacks.

Such unrest among the nations of the world places a
heavy strain on international relations. Which parties in
the struggle deserve support, which should be discouraged?
A nation's leaders are hard pressed to make decisions that
will work both for national security and the world's welfare. Shall missionaries be asked to withdraw from the
countries where they serve during periods of crisis? Can
more refugees from distressed nations be received and
given a new home? In many such ways, the world's turmoil
and the Christian mission impinge on one another.

TRANSITIONS IN THE CHURCH

Churches in "mission lands," their members having
breathed the fresh air of national freedom, today are asking
for a loosening of the ties that have bound them closely to
mission boards and overseas influences. They want to be at
liberty to make their own decisions. They want their own
people to be the leaders in the church. They still desire
and need help in the forms of money and personnel, but
they want to determine how the money and the missionaries will be employed.

Far-sighted mission boards have planned and worked for
this day of independence among new churches. But its
coming does not magically solve the problems of relationship between church and mission. The churches of the
world need one another, each for those resources in Christ
that the others may have in greater measure. However, just

as relationships in a family are not easy, even where strong
ties of love exist, so problems of authority, responsibility,
mutual respect, and equality of partnership require wisdom,
love, and tact among the churches.

The Christian mission at home also faces social upheaval.
North American society, too, is in turmoil. Huge metropoli-
tan areas are developing at a faster rate than the church, or
even municipal services. One out of every five persons
moves every year. Population expansion and mobility present a variety of problems to the churches. In one area,
the problem might be ministering to an expanding community; in another, it might be serving a diminishing population; in yet another, adopting a program for a community
whose ethnic or economic character has markedly changed.

The Christian church must be sensitive to our complex,
secularized society, with its religious pluralism and its in-
tricacies of social and civil structures. The issue of separation of church and state remains troublesome. Shall federal
aid be given to religious or private schools, as well as public
schools? Is equal freedom guaranteed to persons of all
faiths? The church must maintain a creative balance between freedom and responsibility. It must find ways to express itself relevantly on national issues while preserving its
freedom of conscience and decision.

Some of the tokens of the new day are in the church itself. Until recently, the history of the church has been one
of continuing division and fragmentation. One denomination after another was established, especially in freedom-
honoring nations, and each denomination sent out its own

missionaries. This tendency is diminishing in the twentieth century, and co-operation in missionary work has increased. In Asia and Africa, however, co-operation has not been enough. Where Christians are a very small minority, unity sometimes becomes a necessity for survival. As a consequence, many denominational lines have been obliterated in Asia and Africa by the creation of united churches. In some places, missionaries were under instructions from the beginning to establish national churches without organizational ties to a church in Europe or North America. Another sign of the trend toward unity has been the forming of strong Christian councils to provide instruments of co-operation and fellowship between denominations. The ties between church groups within such councils may be stronger than their denominational ties to church bodies on another side of the world, since the councils combine the resources of the churches for the evangelization of their own lands.

In Canada and in the United States, the Canadian Council of Churches and the National Council of Churches of Christ have been developed for just this sort of purpose. Growing co-operation through them is imperative if the mission of Christ is to have a chance against the gigantic challenges of population growth, mobility, urbanization, and secularization. Some church bodies, seeking to strengthen Christianity's response to these challenges, have joined forces. The United Church of Canada, The Methodist Church, The Evangelical United Brethren Church, The United Church of Christ, The United Presbyterian Church,

U.S.A., and The American Lutheran Church are examples of recent unions.

Elsewhere in the world, regional associations of Christians are developing. The East Asia Christian Conference is a pioneering example, as it helps to give Christian minorities in Asia a sense of unity in their almost overwhelming task. The conference was brought into being primarily to serve as an organization through which Asian churches may help one another in the fulfillment of mission. An all-African church conference is in process of formation. Similar associations may develop in Latin America, the Middle East, and other regions.

Such developments among the churches of these lands are signs of vitality and growth. But they require changes in relationships with the churches of other lands, adjustments such as those affecting the status of missionaries and the use of funds. We in local churches need to understand what is happening between church groups in our country and those in other nations if we are to fill our roles in the world mission effectively.

Describing the new day in mission, Bishop Newbigin says: "The Church's mission is concerned with the ends of the earth. When that dimension is forgotten, the heart goes out of the business. There will never be a great response to the call for missionary service, unless it is recognisably related to that ultimate horizon. We have noted that in an earlier day this 'ends of the earth' dimension was present simply in the fact that the missionary went from Europe or America to parts of the earth which were—from the point

of view of the sending churches—'regions beyond.' We have
to face the fact that we have left that era completely be-
hind. We are now required by the facts to look at the missionary enterprise from a completely new point of view—
from the point of view of the world-wide Church. The
home-base is everywhere—wherever the Church is."[3]

Bishop Newbigin goes on to say that Tokyo may still be
the "ends of the earth" to Boston, but that Boston is also
the "ends of the earth" from the point of view of Christians in Tokyo. Hence, either place is a mission field. There
is a missionary task on every man's doorstep. But we do not
discharge our duty as Christians fully unless we are involved in the task on our own doorstep, and also in some
other part of the total world-wide task.

THE GRACE OF RECEIVING

The churches of North America need to make an adjustment that they may not readily realize and that is difficult
to make. They should open themselves to help from Christians in other parts of the world. Those Christians have
gifts of the gospel to share with people in Canada and the
United States that are to be welcomed and received gra-
ciously.

Some denominations have already begun the practice of
receiving fraternal workers from other lands, finding it a
rewarding experience in missionary partnership. In un-

---

[3] Newbigin, Lesslie. *One Body, One Gospel, One World: The Christian Mission Today.* London, Eng.: International Missionary Council,
1958, pp. 27-28.

official ways, this reciprocal ministry is accomplished by the visits of Christian leaders from other lands, who preach in North American pulpits, teach in university and seminary classrooms, and counsel and encourage their Canadian and American colleagues. The thousands of Christian overseas students, on university campuses and on visits to homes on this continent, contribute to this reciprocal missionary influence. We of the West must open our minds and our hearts more fully and more humbly to this greatly needed ministry among us.

The dynamic situation in the world mission of the church requires that every congregation understand its place in that mission. What may have seemed like adequate motivation and response in the past is probably no longer so. Each church and each Christian must listen to what the gospel and the times have to say.

4

The Mission in
Congregational Life

A GROUP OF MEN AND WOMEN WHO WERE leaders in the congregation were planning the calendar of a Baptist church in a Midwestern suburb. In a moment of relaxation, someone asked how many of them had grown up in a Baptist church. As it turned out, the questioner was the only one. All the rest were Methodist, Presbyterian, Congregationalist, or Lutheran.

We can make two observations about this incident. It enlarges the point made about mobility in the preceding chapter: moving from place to place often results in families' changing their denominational connections.

It also shows that the transition from one kind of church to another isn't particularly difficult. There was enough familiarity about the functions of the Baptist church to let these men and women quickly find their way to leadership.

All of us have had enough experience in churches other

than our own to know that the basic aspects of congregational life are much alike. This is not surprising. Every congregation, no matter what its affiliation, is called to do the will of its Lord. Seeking to live and work in obedience to the same purpose, congregations would naturally develop the same broad functions.

A sound program of education for mission requires an understanding of these functions of congregational life. Obviously, if a church exists for mission, its functions must serve mission.

WORSHIP

One essential dimension of a congregation's life is corporate worship. We gather each week to relate our lives to God through Christ in reverence and hope. In the worship service, we open ourselves to the activities of the Spirit of God. The church building itself is an instrument toward that end. It is God's house, constructed not merely as a shelter from the elements but so that its beauty might help turn our thoughts to God.

The Word of God, read and preached, calls us to listen for the eternal word that God desires to speak. In hymn and prayer, we express our praise of God, our penitence for sin, our confidence and dedication. Pre-eminently in the observance of the Lord's Supper, we confess, in the presence of God and with all generations of disciples, fealty to Christ, our Savior and Lord. The dimension of worship is deep and essential, an activity from which all other aspects of Christian life move out with power and meaning.

TEACHING

Christian teaching is another dimension of our congregation's life. We have the responsibility of nurturing one another in the Christian life, guiding persons to a vital faith in God through Christ, and encouraging them to grow constantly in grace and knowledge. Such nurture encompasses all Christian virtues and duties, so that every person may have a chance to grow to full maturity of mind and spirit. This education is the primary responsibility of Christian homes, but the church supplements the teaching of the home and as far as possible makes up for the lack where families fail.

In this function, the congregation invests the time of many leaders and teachers. The congregation plans a curriculum that, through activities, materials, and face to face contact of teachers with learners and learners with one another, prepares the way for spiritual growth. The minister, or a member of his staff, gives much time to education. He supervises the total program and conducts classes to prepare persons for church membership or to train teachers for their task. Since parents are expected to provide much Christian nurture by daily example, informal instruction, and family worship, the church devotes considerable energy to strengthening the family life of its members.

FELLOWSHIP

A third dimension of experience in the congregation is Christian fellowship. Our fellowship as church members probes deeply into the spiritual realities of our Christian faith. It catches up all our intimate contacts in work and prayer, through which we acknowledge and strengthen our reliance on one another in the bonds of Christian love. In fact, it springs from the fellowship we have in Christ and with Christ. This deeper spiritual experience of fellowship expresses itself in many ways—concern for one another, pleasant associations, social occasions, informal visiting.

These familiar examples are signposts, marking for us how good it is for believers to dwell together in unity. A few decades ago, this aspect of congregational life seemed more obvious and essential than in contemporary society. We may remember communities where the church provided most of the opportunities for social life. Adults heard and discussed the news there. Young people found much of their recreation there. It was the true center of its community. Now school, club, television, automobile—all have diminished the dependence of people on the church for their social fulfillment. In a society that is surfeited with opportunities for fellowship—whose individual members are so frequently fleeing from themselves—the congregation has the unique role of relating us to one another in Christian love.

The aspects of congregational life that we have considered contribute to the growth and development of the congregation itself. Worship, teaching, and fellowship strengthen our congregation so it may be prepared to perform its mission. Every living organism depends on such internal care. Our human bodies require food and rest and healing to stay alive. So it is with our church.

EVANGELISM

But neither our bodies nor our church remain healthy when pampered and coddled. Only vigorous exercise, challenging duty, and stern discipline keep them fit. There are some aspects of congregational life that indicate whether a church is a vital force in a community or whether, grown fat, it is content to sit in a rocking chair and hum hymns across its paunch.

Take the dimension of evangelism, for example. The congregation ought to direct other people into faith in Jesus Christ and thereby into the fellowship of the church. Such activity, leading persons from unbelief to belief, touches the very heart of the Christian gospel.

In this aspect of the church's duty, we confront people face to face in overt Christian witness. Two-by-two, in New Testament style, we may visit in homes of the community, making Jesus Christ known there. The preaching of the gospel proclaims Christ. Evangelism is a quality of congregational life, making known the presence of the living Christ in many ways, not only in primarily evangelistic activities.

The very presence of the church in its community speaks of its Lord. The church building as a physical symbol and the congregation as a living organism remind people of the presence of God among them. The preaching and teaching of the gospel week by week make this witness vocal and persuasive. Guided by God's Holy Spirit the church prays, visits, affirms, and invites, introducing persons to the Living Lord of the church and leading them to faith in him.

SERVICE

The congregation reaches beyond itself into its community to serve in critical areas of need. Social evils such as racial prejudice, poverty, crime, and juvenile delinquency challenge the church to constructive action in the name of its holy God. It is called to lead social advance for the welfare of men.

The church should recognize the powers and prerogatives of government in these activities. It should also understand the role of civic and secular organizations that exist for community betterment. In fact, the church fulfills much of its responsibility in this area through its members performing their civic and social duties in the spirit of Christ. Yet the church must also make its corporate witness known in legitimate ways and by appropriate actions.

Such service done in the name of Christ is motivated by a deep love for people. It is the cup of cold water Jesus praised. A church sees a need and responds generously and sacrificially, after the example of the Lord himself. Its ultimate goal is evangelism; its immediate motivation arises from the need that cries out for loving service or courageous reform.

MISSION AND MISSIONS

The Christian mission is another aspect of congregational life that leads a church outside itself. When we speak of *the mission* of the church we mean its calling to fulfill the purposes of its Lord in the world. We refer to *missions* as

those specific means by which the congregation seeks to
join other Christians in accomplishing that mission everywhere in the world. The work of *missions* is the means by
which *the mission* is given its clearest visibility in the world.

Undoubtedly the foreign missions and home missions
projects about which we have heard from childhood come
to mind first: a new church in Thailand, a hospital in Ken-
tucky, religious broadcasting in Japan, Spanish schools in
New Mexico, schools and churches for Indian reservations.
Such activities have inspired the church to give itself sacrificially for the work of Christ's kingdom in all parts of the
world.

But the dimension of Christian mission leads beyond
these concepts until the congregation sees that no land is
foreign to God. The mission possesses the same essential
nature whether in Minnesota or Malaya, in Tennessee or
Tanganyika. The crossing of boundaries is the important
thing—proclaiming the gospel, the good news in Jesus
Christ, on every frontier and doing it in co-operation with
other Christians. We may find the frontier across the rail-
road tracks, as near as the church's threshold, or twelve
thousand miles away. We may recognize it in human need
without reference to geography at all. The frontier, wherever it stands, calls for the response of Christian missions.

THE PARTS AND THE WHOLE

Obviously, the dimensions of our congregational life do
not exist separate and distinct from one another. For example, missions receives from all the rest and contributes

to them all. The dimension of worship should unite our congregation with every other congregation, and with the eternal purpose of Christ's mission. We dramatize the relationship between worship and missions when we observe World Wide Communion Sunday or World Day of Prayer, beginning as they do with services on Tonga, in the Pacific, and following the course of the sun until it sets on a tiny island off the coast of Alaska.

Fellowship and missions intertwine inextricably; fellowship in Christ extends from our congregation to the whole Christian family. Evangelism and service provide the core of missionary outreach; wherever the Christian seeks to fulfill his mission, he invites persons to relationship of faith in Jesus Christ and serves them in Christ's name.

Missions and education relate to one another inevitably. All our Christian education effort moves toward preparing persons for their participation in mission, and our missionary program contains large elements of teaching.

Interrelated though the dimensions of congregational life may be, they need to be considered separately so that each may be performed faithfully and intelligently. Thus mission and missions, though in one sense they comprehend the whole life and purpose of the church, need to be seen as composing that particular compelling motive that leads the church out to every frontier of need where the gospel is to be proclaimed.

Our congregation is part of a denomination, and that denomination maintains mission boards whose task is to administer missionary outreach for it. These agencies super-

vise missionary programs on frontiers of our national life—
for example, in the troubled areas of great cities—where
no congregation or group of congregations could accomplish the task. They develop and maintain relationships
with the churches in other lands, sending them the people
and resources that will be of most help to them. They dis-
patch representatives to proclaim the gospel and establish
the church where no church exists. They engage in co-
operative church planning for carrying the gospel to the
cities and the open countryside; they develop specialized
technical ministries in the areas of medicine, education,
agriculture, and literacy.

To these activities of mission, the boards call local
churches for participation and support. These forms of outreach are "the ends of the earth" for the local congregation,
whose mission is on its own doorstep and across all boundaries of need.

EDUCATING THE CONGREGATION FOR MISSION

Every congregation must be provided with clear opportunities to understand and undertake the missionary obligations of the church. This is the duty of missionary education
—education for mission.

Education for mission is the obligation of the congregation's administrative council or session, under the leadership of the minister. It deserves and requires no less than
the authority and concern of the official body that supervises the total program of the church. Consequently, this
council or session should oversee the assignment to leaders

and committees of responsibility for education for mission. It should provide sufficient financial resources in the church's budget for an effective missionary education program. During specific activities in the program, the official board should use its influence to encourage their success.

The congregation will probably have a committee or board of Christian education to which falls responsibility for the total educational program of the church. Its members will represent all the age-groups and educational activities of the church. In this Christian education committee lies a large part of the responsibility for the missionary education effort.

Many churches form a committee specifically for missionary education, usually as a sub-committee of the official board or of the Christian education committee. Its membership and duties depend on the congregation's organization. This committee should include representatives of all groups that have an interest in or responsibility for missionary education—church school, women's society, men's organization, youth groups, missions or outreach commission, deacons. It should co-ordinate all the activities carried on in a program of education for mission. Obviously, its members should be persons who can devote enough time to guarantee the congregation an effective program.

We need to be aware of a danger in establishing this special committee. It should not lead anyone to conclude that its program belongs to a few individuals or the groups they represent. The mission of the church includes every Christian. Means should be found to involve every church

member in it. Education for mission is essential for everyone, because participation in the Christian mission is essential for every one.

In some churches in the past, the mission of the church was
considered an interest of women alone. The men kept their
hands off and the women did a work that won praise and
admiration. In today's world, however, the mission is ham-
pered by such an allocation of responsibility. Our congregation's activities in education for mission should be an integral part of the total education and interpretation program of the church, for the participation of the entire
membership.

5

Christian Education and Education for Mission

DURING THE LAST YEARS OF THE NINETEENTH
century, the missionary enterprise of the churches of
North America reached large proportions. The Student
Volunteer Movement had been organized and was recruit-
ing many college students for missionary service overseas.
In order to keep the flame of interest burning among them
and to provide them with more information about missionary work, a number of denominations created an interdenominational organization in 1902. This organization,
The Young People's Missionary Movement, produced study
materials and conducted conferences on the mission of the
church. Church leaders saw that this kind of program also
was a means by which local churches could learn more
about missionary work and thus support it more intelligently
and generously. The organization soon broadened its oper-
ations under the name, the Missionary Education Move-

ment of the United States and Canada (familiarly, MEM).

When the National Council of the Churches of Christ in the United States of America was formed, this co-operative activity was continued in the Commission on Missionary Education. Denominations in Canada maintained their participation and also developed their own interdenominational organization, the Committee on Missionary Education of the Canadian Council of Churches.

During the years since 1902, the denominations of the two nations have themselves enlarged their missionary education programs and efforts, incorporating in them the use of the plans and materials they have produced co-operatively through Friendship Press, the publishing name for the Commission on Missionary Education.

DEFINING THE TERMS

During the same period when "missionary education" was becoming a familiar phrase among them, the churches also developed use of the term "Christian education." This aspect of organized church life began with the Sunday school movement. As denominations created programs of Christian nurture that extended beyond the Sunday school and as they prepared supporting educational materials, they adopted the term Christian education to describe what they were doing.

Nevin Harner and David Baker, in *Missionary Education in Your Church,* defined missionary education as "the sum of all our efforts to cultivate in children, young people, and adults a Christlike concern for people of every class, race, and nation; an intimate knowledge of how the Christian fellowship is being extended both at home and abroad; and a hearty participation in all endeavors to enlarge this fellowship of Christian faith and brotherhood until it covers the earth."[1]

Christian education is understood to be education into the Christian life. It introduces persons to knowledge about God, about man and his relation to God, the Bible, the church, and the meaning of the Christian life. But it gives knowledge only so as to touch the person's whole life, leading him to want to do the will of God, to have a Christian attitude toward himself and others, to work and pray for the establishing of Christ's kingdom, and to be a living witness to the gospel in both word and deed.

Christian leaders are continually trying to improve their understanding and definition of the objective of Christian education. A recent statement affirms that the objective of Christian education is "that all persons be aware of God through his self-disclosure, especially his redeeming love as revealed in Jesus Christ, and that they respond in faith and love—to the end that they may know who they are and what their human situation means, grow as sons of God rooted in the Christian community, live in the Spirit of God in every relationship, fulfilling their common discipleship in the world, and abide in the Christian hope."

Clearly this purpose of Christian education is the aim of the whole church for every person in its fellowship. Chris-

[1] Harner, Nevin C. and Baker, David D. *Missionary Education in Your Church.* New York: Friendship Press, 1950, p. 19.

tian education exists, not for purposes of its own, but for
the sake of the mission of the church. Education for mission finds its place in this comprehensive understanding of
the educational task of the church.

EDUCATION FOR MISSION

Education for Mission is the title of this book and in
many places it is used as a synonym for missionary education. It indicates that the objective of this special area of
the church's educational responsibility is to help persons respond in faith and love to God through Jesus Christ by fulfilling their discipleship in the Christian mission. As Christians, each of us should understand Christ's mission as it
applies to us and to the whole world. We are called to involve ourselves in mission where we live and, as much as
possible, in every other part of the world. What we learn
about the mission of the church elsewhere will instruct us
in our own Christian duty. Our involvement in mission in
our own community will lead us to a concern for the mission everywhere.

An important part of education for mission must be education about missions—about the projects and programs by
which the churches seek to fulfill their responsibility at
home and around the world. The churches have developed
an extensive missionary program. North American churches
in the co-operative movement had in 1960 more than ten
thousand missionaries working in fraternal fellowship with
Christians overseas, in addition to the many performing
similar service in the homeland. Similarly, churches in Asia,

for example, had sent more than two hundred missionaries to work with Christians in lands other than their own.

This work needs the support of Christian people in terms of intelligent understanding, prayer, personnel, and money. Such support grows out of effective education and motivation. At this point, education and promotion are closely allied.

As far as a local congregation is concerned, we can carry on education for mission without too much concern about distinguishing between education and promotion. It will help us in working with our denominations, however, to realize that some of them separate the two functions in the organization of their work. There are agencies for Christian education or missionary education, and there are agencies for united promotion or mission interpretation. Of course, complete separation of these functions is impossible. Promotion or interpretation, which may seek for immediate response in action or financial giving, also teaches—if it is consistent with the long-range goals and principles of education. Education, on the other hand, always tests itself by its fruits but does not disregard the desire for immediate evidences of growth. For these reasons, persons concerned for education and those concerned for promotion and interpretation are both engaged in educating church members for mission.

Attention to specific missionary projects and activities should always be related to the total Christian mission. An effective missionary education program will lead persons beyond an interest in one area or one kind of work to an awareness of world mission strategy. It will guide them to understand the transitions occurring in missionary work. Church members, for example, who for years have supported a favorite school in Malaya, will need to understand why the church may have closed it or turned it over to government control. Those whose favorite missionary may have been transferred from one country to another, or may even have been left at home without a new assignment, must see the issues that brought about such a decision by the board of missions or the overseas church. In all possible ways, church members need an education that helps them respond affirmatively, in attitude and action, to the mission's dynamic nature, bursting as it is these days with new occasions and new duties.

THE PLACE OF EDUCATION FOR MISSION

How then is education for mission to be related to the total task of Christian education? How is it to be kept from fencing itself off as a separate activity? If education for mission were distinct and separate, could it then be added or detached at will? And if so, could mission or missions be disregarded as not belonging intrinsically to the total life and work of the church? To ask these questions is to imply their answers. Christian education and education for mission are not two competing or conflicting interests. Education for mission is one element in the total spectrum of Christian education, and in the total life of the church, lifted up so that it may receive proper attention.

We have already mentioned the teaching function of a

congregation. James Smart in *The Teaching Ministry of the Church,* makes its importance unmistakably clear: "The Church of Jesus Christ has, of necessity, a teaching function. The Church must teach, just as it must preach, or it will not be the Church. . . . Teaching belongs to the essence of the Church and a church that neglects this function of teaching has lost something that is indispensable to its nature as a church. It is a defective church if it is lacking at this point, just as a church in which the gospel ceases to be preached in its purity or a church in which the sacraments cease to be rightly administered is a defective church."[2] And we might add, a church in which mission is not an essential characteristic is defective.

OPPORTUNITIES FOR EDUCATION

The primary opportunity for education in the church program is the Sunday church school. Hardly a unit of study in the graded materials for the church school does not have some bearing on the Christian mission. Any activity that guides boys and girls into more meaningful and helpful relations with others, that develops in them an acceptance of responsibility for sharing the gospel, is education for mission. In addition, extended sessions of the church school, weekday released-time classes, and vacation church schools provide excellent opportunities for the missionary education of children. Any experience of youth that helps them identify themselves with others in doing the will of God

[2] Smart, James. *The Teaching Ministry of the Church.* Philadelphia: The Westminster Press, 1954, p. 11.

and bringing others into a redemptive relationship with Jesus Christ is education for mission. Any occasion for relating adults to the ministry of the church in all ages and in all places makes possible education for mission.

If teachers of the church school are to avail themselves of these opportunities, they must themselves understand the missionary nature of the church. They must be equipped with resources that will help them enlarge the experience and understanding of their pupils. Thus one aspect of education for mission is selecting, training, motivating, and providing resources for teachers and leaders of the church school.

In most churches, the young people come together in evening groups as well as in Sunday morning church school. The discussion topics and projects for the evening meetings frequently center around problems and areas of current youth experience. Here, too, is a constant opportunity to build the concept of Christian mission into the growing Christian maturity of young people. Many of the immediate problems with which they deal are those of Christian mission right in their own communities, and these reflect the human needs and problems to which the Christian mission is addressed in any part of the world.

Women's organizations have traditionally had a special interest in missions. Many denominational women's programs began in earlier days as missionary societies. Though many of them have broadened their scope to include the total Christian experience, women groups still have a very lively concern for the missionary activity of the church.

Their attention to devotional life, Bible study, service, and fellowship is enriched by concern for the world mission of the church.

Organized men's programs may also be a means of education that is clearly missionary in character. Because of their interest in world affairs and their work, which in modern times is likely to have international ramifications, men may discover new understanding of their roles in the world mission of the church.

Not the least among the teaching opportunities in the church is the teaching ministry of the pastor. From his pulpit, in his visiting, in his administration of the church program, and in occasions of small group study and discussion, the minister has a responsibility to teach his congregation in ways that will undergird their commitment to the mission.

Usually it is the minister's personal responsibility to teach catechetical or church membership classes of children, youth, and adults who are being prepared for confirmation or for acceptance into full rights and obligations of the congregation. One of the important areas of Christian understanding for persons at this critical juncture is mission and missions. By his teaching and influence here the minister can help to mold the life of his congregation.

So the educational program of the church provides limitless opportunities for education for mission. Indeed, the education comes to its fulfillment when it lays a firm foundation for missionary involvement. This is the educational duty of the church; it should be accomplished for the very reason that the church is missionary by nature and inevitably missionary in its teaching.

FAILURE, UNLESS . . .

Yet there are many churches where facilities are ideal, where materials are excellent, where teachers are well-trained, but where missionary zeal and vision are absent. Such situations fall short of the Christian standard. They show unmistakably that, without clear attention by leaders and program, the missionary duty of the Christian recedes into vague and indifferent response.

If education for mission is to be effective, certain persons must assume it as their chief responsibility. It is the concern of all Christians, and it should be planned to involve as many people as possible, but a core of devoted, trained leaders must take the initiative. Every function of the church needs its leaders. In the New Testament church, Paul described this division of function, suggesting that Christ's gifts were that "some should be apostles, some prophets, some evangelists, some pastors and teachers." In a twentieth century congregation, some must be leaders in mission and education for mission.

An adequate program of Christian education also requires periods of special concentration when the mission of the church is brought into sharp focus for the congregation, or any of its groups. Such learning experiences are frequently based on annual themes, selected interdenominationally and supported by interdenominationally published materials. The themes create an opportunity for congregations of many denominations to pursue the same area of study and to unite in occasions of leadership development and community activity.

Frequently these occasions for missionary education are provided by units of study in the Sunday morning or evening curriculum, or by elective units suggested to study groups for their exploration. In increasing number, denominations and their congregations are developing schools of missions or church family nights for giving special attention to the missionary activity of the church. These programs have the advantage of making it possible for families to be together in an experience of worship and study, with graded activities as part of the program.

A vacation church school, a weekday class, or a Sunday morning extended session offer an excellent opportunity for concentrating entirely on a mission study unit with children. It is possible in these circumstances to include projects or excursions that give the learning experiences creativity and reality. Mission themes give attractive substance to the program of the whole vacation school when several grades are involved.

In addition to organized efforts in education for mission, a church can always keep the missionary motive of its work before its members by exhibits, displays, book tables, and special notices. Churches should use more imagination in focusing attention on some special interest or occasion by an attractive exhibit. They are often outdone by public schools, libraries, or other secular institutions. The life and work of the church around the world provides an excellent subject for such indirect teaching. "A picture is worth a thousand words," but only if it is placed where it can be seen.

Whether people are reading more or less since the advent of television, one thing cannot be denied—the publishing of books continues to increase. Someone buys books, and of all those who ought to keep abreast of the times, Christian people should. One unlimited opportunity to accomplish education for mission is to encourage people to read the publications made available to them on the missionary work of the church.

To sum up, education for mission is integral to the structure of every church. It must be provided for. It should be a concern of the minister and the church's official council. It should be a specific interest of the church's board or committee on Christian education. It should be the chief responsibility of a special group of informed and dedicated leaders.

6

Education for Mission in
the Curriculum

A FEW YEARS AGO, A FAMILY WAS FACED
with moving to another part of their state. They finally
selected a community where they could attend a church
of their denomination. One of the advantages was that the
familiarity of the denomination's church school curriculum
would help their children adjust readily to new teachers
and new classrooms.

Curriculum is an important element in Christian education. It is, in essence, a plan to ensure that the growing experiences of children, youth, and adults over a period of
years of consecutive study will lead them to a mature
Christian faith.

Curriculum provides for learning situations and resources.
It consists of more than printed lesson materials. "It is a
living experience of persons in Christian fellowship as they
confront God and seek to know and do his will, under the

guidance of Christian teachers."[1] Its context is the Christian community—the church. It is implemented by the worshiping, witnessing, nurturing fellowship of Christians. The learner enters into this fellowship, himself a part of the context of the curriculum. As he engages in learning experiences, the Holy Spirit works in him and in the church to accomplish his growth as a Christian.

While the church cannot limit or direct the work of the Spirit, it can facilitate the response of persons to him. Printed materials for teaching and learning are the means, among others, by which this response is achieved. Each denomination prepares materials for a specified course or courses, made up of units of work dealing with various aspects of the total Christian education objective.

It is impossible to deal comprehensively here with missionary education opportunities in all the curricula of the denominations. While there is a basic similarity in them— because of the common faith and education goals they share—there are great differences in the way their plans are organized. This book can only illustrate and suggest the opportunities; local church leaders and teachers will be able to work out the specific applications to their own work.

CURRICULA PLANNED CO-OPERATIVELY

A number of denominations organize their curricula on the basis of a design or resource units that they have developed co-operatively. From this curriculum design they pre-

[1] Vieth, Paul H. *The Church School.* Philadelphia: Christian Education Press, 1957, p. 69.

pare their own lesson treatments and materials for pupils and teachers. Each denomination injects into the units of study any ideas and information called for by the needs and interests of its own people.

The plan has provided units of study in the various age groups based on interdenominational mission study themes of the year. It has been the custom for the denominations, through the interdenominational Commission on Missionary Education, to select a home and a foreign mission study theme for each year. Selected four or five years in advance, these themes can enter into denominational preparation of curriculum materials. Of course, other units also deal with the general topic of the mission of the church, even though they are not related specifically to the interdenominational themes.

The curriculum of one denomination will illustrate how mission study units, based on the interdenominational themes, are made a part of the Sunday church school plan. In this denomination, when Africa was the overseas theme, the January lessons for the senior youth were *Why Africa, Africa Today, The People of Africa,* and *Partners in Christian Vocation.* The unit for primary children in the group graded lessons was on *A Christian Family in Africa,* while the unit for juniors dealt with *The Church in the Congo.*

Among four possible series of studies for adults, the unit of exploration proposed in the Adult Fellowship Series for January included topics on *Africa Awakening, The Church at Work in the Congo, Rural Africa, Industrial Africa,* and *Africa in the World.* Using these lessons and their supplementary resources, adults were helped to see the role of the Christian mission in one part of the world.

Throughout all age groups, the Africa theme was treated in ways appropriate to the experience and needs of the persons involved. In each case, the interdenominational materials were recommended as resources for preparing the teachers and for enriching the learning experiences of the pupils. In the children's lessons, projects and activities were proposed, some of which required the use of the specialized missionary education materials that this denomination had joined with others to produce co-operatively.

These particular units in the Sunday church school, being based on a missionary study theme, had the advantage of unusually rich supplementary resources readily at the teachers' hands. In this way, education for mission was advanced among the many persons enrolled in Sunday church school classes—the most extensive educational program most congregations have.

Such specific units on the home or overseas mission of the church in any one year are by no means the only time or way in which the mission of the church is treated. Throughout the units of study year after year, there are explorations into the life and teachings of Jesus, the history of the church, the work and ministry of the church, and the redeeming purposes of God in the world. These subjects bear fundamentally and sharply on the Christian missionary effort.

Teachers should be alert for these opportunities. Furthermore, they need abundant resources near at hand to help them make the most of every teaching situation. Almost subconsciously and yet very convincingly, every Christian ought to come to an understanding of mission and the missionary work of the church as a part of the integrity of all Christian experience and responsibility. The church school curriculum is planned in the hope of achieving this goal for as many churchgoers in as many different situations as possible.

CURRICULA PLANNED DENOMINATIONALLY

In recent years, some denominations have developed new curricula, seeking to improve the teaching function of their churches by providing an educational program carefully tailored to denominational situations. One such curriculum design is called the Pilgrim Series or the Church and Home Series. It is built around four main areas of understanding and experience: *Commitment to Christ, Understanding the Bible, The Christian Church and Its Work,* and *Christian Living.* These areas in turn are divided into a three-year cycle of quarterly units so that every department in the church school is working in the same general area at the same time.

Of this plan, it is said that "missionary education is not a thing apart, but warp and woof of the curriculum itself. While there are particular courses of study that deal quite directly with the outreach of the church to people in other lands or special groups in our own country, no line can be drawn sharply between so-called missionary education courses and other courses. The mission of the church is included in every other course."² This curriculum is being replaced by a new one, in which the same principle of integration will be maintained.

The courses most clearly identifiable as education for mission are contained in the sections on *The Christian Church and Its Work*. The theme for one quarter is *How the Church Grows,* and in that quarter, for example, third and fourth graders study *The Story Goes Round the World,* while junior highs have as their concern, *Our Church Around the World.* In another quarter, seniors study *After the Apostles,* and older young people and adults consider *Our Common Protestant Heritage,* a significant part of which is the heritage of the missionary enterprise.

For such explicit units on the Christian mission as these, teachers are directed to the resources in their church libraries or to their denominational publishing houses. In the case of the third and fourth grade unit on *The Story Goes Round the World,* the teacher is advised to secure the interdenominational Friendship Press publications, *The Round Window,* by Elizabeth Allstrom and *Many Hands in Many Lands,* by Alice Geer Kelsey. These books contain stories from all parts of the world. Missionary biographies, stories, background resource books, maps, and projected audio-visuals are available to provide bountiful help for the teacher and the class.

But education for mission is not involved solely where

² "Pilgrim Series and the Mission of the Church." Boston, Mass.: The Division of Christian Education, Congregational Christian Churches [leaflet, 1958].

the theme of the unit makes it explicit. In the two quarters that deal with the life of Jesus, the curriculum is obviously laying a foundation for understanding the missionary nature of the Christian faith. For example, in the course, *Stories Jesus Told*, third and fourth graders learn the meaning of service from the life of a famous missionary. The junior high courses include accounts of the way Jesus' followers traveled over the world to tell his story. In another quarter, junior high and senior high studies about Paul open up excellent avenues for discussion of the Christian's missionary vocation. In fact, there is a missionary application to almost every unit.

Projects and activities suggested in the various units help children feel that they belong to a fellowship of people who know God's love and express it in acts of love toward other people. Small children will not grasp the idea of the church as mission, nor will they understand very much about what missionaries really are. But they can come to know what it is to be part of the church. And they can develop a feeling that the church expresses concern for other people. Youth and adults can participate in more specific stewardship projects and in opportunities for service with full understanding and commitment. Many places in the whole curriculum propose such involvement.

The missionary education program of this denomination, as of others, recommends the interdenominational materials for extended sessions of the Sunday church school, for weekday released-time sessions, and for vacation church school classes. In this way, further experiences in understanding Christian mission supplement and enrich the Pilgrim Series. The denomination also recommends mission literature for individual or family reading at home.

Another such curriculum is the Christian Faith and Life Series, which also follows a three-year cycle. It deals in consecutive years with *Jesus Christ, The Bible,* and *The Church.* Children's, youth, and adult lessons follow the same general theme for the year, making possible family study and worship and providing a unity of experience throughout the church school. In each of the three years of the cycle, units of learning occur that are directly concerned with the Christian mission. Other units frequently have indirect and supporting relationship to mission. While none of the units can directly relate to the interdenominational study themes because of the nature of the plan and of the materials published for the churches' use, specific missionary education publications are recommended as supplementary resources for teacher and pupil.

The denomination provides a service to the editors of its lesson materials that makes available to them the missionary illustrations, information, and resources they need for developing a curriculum into which mission is thoroughly integrated. As a result the teachers' and pupils' materials contain illuminating references to the missionary outreach of the church.

A few examples from a curriculum of this sort will illustrate those places where mission is most obviously involved. The year in which *The Church* is the theme for all age groups provides useful examples. In one unit in this year's materials, junior children are guided to understand how the Bible was given for everyone. This series of lessons deals very directly with the mission of the church to the whole world. The magazine for children, *World Family,* which describes the mission of the church at home and around the world, is specifically recommended for use during this study. Likewise in this same year, a unit for junior boys and girls deals with *The Secrets of the Faith,* one purpose mentioned being to help juniors "appreciate a faith that withstands persecution and understand that 'the blood of the martyrs is the seed of the church.'"

For primary children in this cycle of lessons, units dealing with what the church does and why Jesus came into the world suggest missionary opportunities. Junior high youth study the beginnings of the church under the theme, *The New People of God.*

For senior high youth, several lessons in the *Church* cycle deal with the subjects, *When Frontiers Beckon* and *Into All World,* studies that directly treat the national and world mission of the Christian church. Similarly a subsequent unit of study turns attention to "indigenous churches around the world." In another unit, junior highs explore the story of the church *In a New World.* The purpose of these lessons is "to help junior highs identify themselves with the situation of American Christians in another era and thus uncover some of their own questions and problems as young members of the church today." This is clearly a study of the history of the mission in America, with missionary implications for the present.

Juniors, in this curriculum, explore a unit titled, *For the Glory of God,* the purpose of which is "to help the junior sense the depth of Christian conviction that brought early settlers to this country and sustained them in trouble."

These random samplings, taken from only one of the three years of this Christian Faith and Life Series curriculum for church and home, indicate again how many are the places where education for mission finds an integral place in the teaching program of the church.

EDUCATION DOESN'T STAND STILL

The development of Christian education curricula is a matter of constant change. The denominations, jointly and separately, continue to study their processes and principles of Christian education and to adjust their curricula to meet the discovered needs. They strive to find ways to relate the permanent elements of the Christian faith and life to the changing circumstances and the deepest needs of human beings. Education for mission must also be dynamic and flexible, finding new patterns consistent with the total education program of the churches in order to bring people into vital involvement in the Christian mission.

The kind of thorough integration of education for mission into the church program illustrated in this chapter requires patient, long-range, deliberate planning, not only by the denomination but by the local church as well. Superficial integration could result in weak education for mission. Carefully planned integration can put mission in proper perspective and give it an effectual foundation. At the beginning of a year in the local church program, the committee on Christian education and its leaders in missionary education need to review thoroughly the curriculum for the year and relate the year's missionary education objectives to it. Teachers may be helped for their role in this task by workers' conferences and by attending mission institutes in the community. They need suggestions and guidance for this particular aspect of their work, as they do for their total task.

It is also important for the leaders to work out clearly the relationship between the educational experiences in mission in the church school curriculum and those special missionary education programs planned for the whole congregation at other times than the Sunday church school. By a systematic plan, every member of the congregation can have the opportunity of a variety of experiences, whose total impact on the church will produce heightened missionary concern. Guidance for such planning is available from the missionary education offices of the denominations.

If teachers are to take the best advantage of their opportunities, good training and ample resources are the prime requisites. Helping them to acquire training and resources is an important responsibility of the special group of leaders who have charge of education for mission for the congregation.

7

Education for Mission in Specialized Programs

"THE CLOSING SESSION WAS MARKED BY AN insistent demand for another school of missions. In response, the pastor promised to give a survey of missions one Sunday night a month until the next school of missions." So reported one church after its first effort at congregation-wide missionary education.

Whether from schools of missions, church family nights, women's meetings, youth fellowship activities, or special study groups, a congregation benefits tremendously from well-planned forms of education for mission beyond the curriculum and schedule of the Sunday church school. The needs of each congregation will indicate what special programs are necessary to provide for every member a meaningful acquaintance with and involvement in the mission. Every such effort, of course, must be developed in relation to the church's total educational program.

THE SCHOOL OF MISSIONS

One of the most popular and effective types of special programs is the family school of missions. It is identified as a series of church family nights on world outreach, a school of world Christianity, a school of Christian fellowship, or in some similar way. A series of consecutive weekly sessions, preferably six and usually in the fall or spring, bring families in the church together to learn about the Christian mission. These may be held on weekday evenings or on Sunday afternoons or evenings. They are sometimes effectively concentrated in a compact week-end program. A light supper, a simple dessert, or other refreshments may be served. Families divide according to age groups for study and activity centering upon the mission study theme. Their leaders are well acquainted with the study program for nursery, kindergarten, primary, junior, junior high, senior high, and adult groups. A closing worship service may be led by one of the families or by one of the age groups.

The school of missions has the advantage of bringing the whole family to the church in a program that reaches youth and children, men and women. The thinking of the entire congregation focuses on missions and world outreach for a period of several days or weeks. Such a school, once or twice a year, helps ensure a well-developed missionary education program for a congregation. The results are deeper understanding and consecration regarding the Christian mission. Church members become informed about the church around the world. They are invigorated by this broadened interest and are led to commit themselves more fully to the mission of the church.

A school of missions creates a sense of fellowship in the missionary enterprise, while enriching the fellowship of the congregation itself. It makes members more informed about stewardship, helping them to know better how to manage the resources that God has entrusted to them. It alerts the congregation to tasks that will stimulate its own growth and development. It gives meaning and purpose to the congregation by helping it discover its mission within the world mission of the church.

The committee responsible for a school of missions will, from the outset, work toward reaching the largest possible number of church members. They will faithfully employ sound educational procedures in all features of the school. Unnecessary organization will be avoided so that the regular activities of the church and the church school are not interrupted. But the committee will work with the care and devotion that the mission of the church deserves.

The schedule of sessions for a school of missions depends on the local circumstances. One schedule that many congregations have found useful is this:

Fellowship Supper	6:15 to 7:00 P.M.
Worship	7:00 to 7:15 P.M.
Study	7:15 to 8:15 P.M.
Assembly	8:15 to 8:45 P.M.
Closing	9:00 P.M.

Any number of variations on this pattern are possible. A school can be held without the fellowship supper, or with the assembly preceding the classes, or with worship and assembly together at the close. One adaptation that provides the same learning opportunities in a school of three weeks as in one lasting five or six is this:

Class sessions	5:30 to 6:30 P.M.
Fellowship supper	6:30 to 7:15 P.M.
Class sessions	7:15 to 8:15 P.M.
Assembly and worship	8:15 to 9:00 P.M.

A SCHOOL'S EDUCATIONAL STANDARDS

To merit the name, a school of missions should meet certain standards. The first, obviously, is educational soundness. For this reason five or six hours of serious class work are recommended, whatever else the program includes. These sessions should be graded, each age group having leadership and learning opportunities geared to the interests and capacities of the persons involved.

Each class or grade should follow a course of study that has unity and progression. It is the responsibility of the leader to ensure these qualities by careful planning and by guiding the experiences of the group, using available resources to create an effective, stimulating learning situation.

Most frequently, the schools follow one of the interdenominational mission study themes and the classes use the interdenominational publications produced for the theme. These materials provide abundant resources for a dynamic encounter with the Christian mission. They include leaders' guides that supply practicable helps to persons who conduct the sessions. Using these themes and materials has the added advantage of permitting interdenominational leadership training. The themes also create a unity of concern and fellowship among neighboring congregations who sponsor schools of missions on the same topics.

Class sessions should not become lecture periods. They ought, instead, to employ methods through which every pupil becomes involved in the learning process. It is a fundamental axiom of education that "you learn best by doing." Educators say that we only remember and use from 25 to 30 per cent of what we hear, 55 per cent of what we hear and see, but from 85 to 90 per cent of what we hear and see and act upon. Obviously, the classes of a school of missions should give every person an opportunity to take part.

Capable leadership is highly important to a school's success. "Choosing teachers was perhaps the most important and hardest job of our planning," one experienced leader has reported. "Poor teachers, poor school; good teachers, good school, regardless of time, place, or materials used. We looked for completely committed, capable, willing workers who accepted the teaching job as an opportunity to do something for God, and to bring missions to the minds and hearts of all pupils. Although our church is not large, we found the teachers, and they learned more than any other group."

Occasions for assembly or worship further enrich a

school of missions. These activities might very well be planned for the entire enrollment; whether younger children, especially primary grades and younger, participate will depend on the nature of the activities.

Group worship brings to the school the awareness of God's presence in its midst and of its dependence on God's Spirit for its understanding of mission. Through worship, the consideration of the Christian mission finds its roots firmly in the Word of God. Prayer unites the persons attending the school with the churches and Christians about whom they are learning and for whom they pray. Each part of the worship experience deserves careful planning and reverent participation so that it will create an expectant attitude among the people for the study and crown the study with holy purpose.

Families who have had time to prepare together may well lead an experience of worship. Or one of the classes may bring to the assembly, in an act of worship, something that has grown out of the class experience.

An assembly period may serve purposes other than worship. A good film or filmstrip on the Christian mission enlivens a meeting. A missionary, prepared to speak to family groups, can bring missions to life, though a congregation cannot always hope to be so fortunate as to have one of the limited number of furloughed missionaries. In any community there are many other persons, qualified by travel, training, or relationships, to give zest to a program. One example is the many overseas students who are attending neighboring colleges and universities. They can be of invaluable help to the school, and the experience of friendly association in a North American church will enrich them, also.

Singing has always characterized the Christian fellowship. Good music inspires. But it is not enough to sing just for the sake of singing. The music should be chosen well, in harmony with the theme of the school. Music or song that comes from or relates to the part of the world or the area of interest indicated by the theme is desirable. Whole families can enjoy music of this sort together and will grow in world consciousness by its use.

PLANNING THE SCHOOL

A school of missions is a large undertaking. It needs capable leadership and careful planning. The committee responsible for it needs to determine objectives, organize resources, and follow a schedule. Such a schedule becomes a check list of the committee's progress. Here is a sample:

_____, first month (six months in advance)
_____ 1. Dates of school set, church calendar cleared.
_____ 2. School of missions committee selected.

_____, second month
_____ 3. Dean or director chosen, theme selected.
_____ 4. Leaders and teachers selected.
_____ 5. Registrar and sub-committee chairmen chosen.
_____ 6. Advance publicity prepared and distributed.

_____, third month
_____ 7. Study materials ordered, audio-visuals booked.
_____ 8. Teaching materials distributed to teachers and leaders.

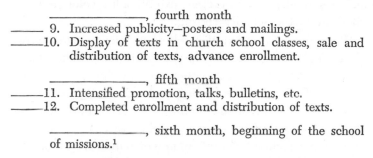

_____, fourth month
_____ 9. Increased publicity—posters and mailings.
_____10. Display of texts in church school classes, sale and distribution of texts, advance enrollment.

_____, fifth month
_____11. Intensified promotion, talks, bulletins, etc.
_____12. Completed enrollment and distribution of texts.

_____, sixth month, beginning of the school of missions.[1]

Leaders and subcommittees accept responsibility for the varied activities of the school. Teachers and leaders of classes have already been mentioned. The *dean* or *director* should be a good administrator, an enthusiastic promoter who will enlist the interest of many people and inspire them with his zeal for the world Christian mission. A *registrar* will take care of advance registrations and see that people are enrolled in their proper classes. A *publicity committee* will have the essential task of bringing the school to the attention of the whole congregation. The school's success will depend largely on how well this committee does its work. A *librarian* will gather textbooks and other resources and make them available to leaders and pupils. A *hospitality* or *fellowship committee* will arrange for meals, provide for guests, and supervise the recreational aspects of the program. Displays and exhibits may be executed by a special committee whose imagination and artistic skill draws together some of the many resources to be found in

[1] *Annual Supplement: Church Schools of Missions,* Missionary Education Department, The United Christian Missionary Society, 1959-60.

any community. An attractive exhibit adds color and excitement to the school's setting.

While this description of a school of missions is in terms of a single congregation, larger parishes, neighborhood churches, groups of congregations of one denomination, or councils of churches are finding such schools a useful form of co-operative missionary education. The Farmingdale-Howell Township Council of Churches, in New York state, for example, conducted a school in which nine congregations participated with a total enrollment of 177 persons from junior high age to adults. The school was self-supporting, ending with a balance that was distributed to the participating churches for missionary purposes. At the close of the school, a nine-month schedule for preparing the next year's program was adopted.

FAMILY NIGHT FELLOWSHIP

Church family nights are similar to a school of missions. In some cases, by denominational plan or local church practice, family nights do not attempt so extensive an educational program as a school of missions. They are often held once a month during one period of the year or another. The span of four weeks between sessions makes the school atmosphere difficult to achieve, disrupting the sequence and continuity of the experience. However, a family night program, by careful planning, can have solid educational value.

If a family night chooses one of the annual mission study themes for the series of evening programs, each program can treat a different aspect of the theme. One or two evenings may be devoted to addresses by competent persons or to panel discussions in which members of the congregation participate. A good film or filmstrip on the mission theme may be the program for another evening. Other interesting features such as drama, music, and exhibits will enrich understanding and appreciation of the theme. The nature of the program will again determine whether the family groups will stay together or whether graded sessions are to be held. Occasions like these are excellent opportunities to bring congregations in touch with missionaries in whom they have a special concern. Interesting extracts from missionaries' letters may be read; accounts of their work may be reported. When available, missionaries appearing in person at the meeting bring missions to the church "in the flesh."

Churches of all sizes and conditions have attempted these programs successfully. A few of them report: "Attendance was limited only by the size of the dining room—325 reservations each week. Others came in after the dinner." "Trouble to prepare? Yes, it is hard work. Time spent? Lots of it. Money for materials? Yes, but they are a good investment." "I believe we should rethink our missionary plans. I didn't know Africa was such an intriguing subject."

Church members sometimes complain, "Our family never has an evening at home." The churches, while professing the conviction that families ought to spend more time together, too often plan so many activities that family life is disrupted. Some churches are attempting to meet this situation by suggesting church family nights at home. They recommend to their families the theme and publications that might have been used in a school of missions or a church family night. Each family is urged to buy one or more of the books and to read them aloud at home. The family may select one of the books best suited to the younger members. Such a plan needs careful preparation, wide announcement, and continuing encouragement of the families so they will follow through on the plans. It can have the wholesome effect of strengthening the church in the home and of uniting the family in a world-wide interest.

At the close of one of these series, a congregation may have a large family festival at the church. This get-together would provide an opportunity for families to share with one another some of the things they have learned or done, by pictures, exhibits, stories, conversation, and fellowship.

THROUGH WOMEN'S ORGANIZATIONS

One of the most effective programs in education for mission beyond the church school curriculum is that carried on by the women's organizations of the churches. In many instances, these organizations have sprung from women's missionary societies. Through them, much mission fervor and activity has been brought into the life of the North American churches. In many denominations, women's organizations now pursue a comprehensive program of activities that include devotional life, stewardship, and social action. Missions is one of their major concerns.

It is common practice among many local women's organizations to divide into circles or small groups for some meetings and activities. These smaller groups meet at times convenient for their members, often in one another's homes. They provide intimate worship, study, discussion, and action.

In the meetings of the whole organization or in circles, a series of studies on the Christian mission one or more times during the year is a stimulating experience. By book review, group discussion, or other presentation, the women of the church come to be familiar with the church's missionary outreach in all parts of the world. Often their knowledge and feeling of involvement are caught up in projects of service and giving. In these they set an example of devoted support of the Christian mission. In fact, their success may sometimes lull the rest of the congregation into a too complacent mood. "Let Georgianna do it," can become the watchword for letting the rest of the congregation ignore its role in mission.

Two aspects of women's programs, in addition to study, deserve mention and commendation. When women's groups create and use guides and calendars for prayer fellowship with Christian leaders and missionaries in all parts of the world, the whole congregation may well participate. Such suggestions for individual or family devotions deserve to be employed faithfully and with understanding by many people. Women's programs of reading also merit the attention of other church members. All the members of the congregation should read books on Christian missions, biographies of missionaries and other church leaders, and the inspiring literature of the Christian faith.

One cannot say enough in praise of the work the women of the church have accomplished. Through their organizations and as individual leaders, dedicated women have set high standards and have given challenging examples to the church. Unfortunately, the church has been slow to grant them opportunities to employ fully their talents and dedication in the whole congregation, outside their own organizational activities.

ORGANIZED MEN'S WORK

Most denominations encourage the organization of the men of the church for certain activities. These men's organizations or brotherhoods propose to enlist the manpower of the church for the total church program. While they usually do not develop an elaborate schedule of activities for the men themselves, the organizations relate the men of the congregation to efforts and circumstances where their resources are needed. Frequently the men of the church have adopted certain projects on behalf of the youth, such as a Boy Scout troop, or for the good of the physical or spiritual welfare of the congregation, like church building improvement or evangelistic visiting. Their activities as an organization are usually monthly meetings, participation in regional or denomination-wide congresses, Communion breakfasts, and similar occasions.

The mission of the church should occupy a place of prominence in these men's activities. With their growing interest and involvement in world affairs by virtue of their occupations, their avocations, and their civic duties, men are more open than ever to an understanding of the contemporary Christian mission. Many have spent several years overseas in military service or in government or business responsibilities. Some of them have had the good fortune of seeing Christian missionary activities overseas. All of them are aware of needs in other parts of the world to which the conscience of the sensitive North American Christian responds.

Some meetings of the men of a congregation could very suitably tie in with their interest in the mission in their own land and in all other parts of the world. These programs should be vigorous and timely. At the same time, the men should be kept informed about publications and other kinds of communications that will sustain and encourage their interest and involvement. Busy men, legitimately contending that they do not have time for many meetings, should at least have time to read several books every year. At least one of these books ought to be on the work of the church around the world. Sunday sermon, adult class discussion, informal conversation, and school of missions complement such reading, enhancing a man's growth.

THE SMALL STUDY GROUP

The informal study group is playing an increasingly significant role in adult education in communities, the YMCA and YWCA, professional groups, and churches. It is a technique that can produce intellectual and spiritual rewards in education for mission. Plentiful resource material is available; all that is necessary is to bring resource and people's interest together.

Study groups of this sort occasionally operate on a short-term basis as part of the Sunday church school program. Or they meet early Sunday evening when the minister can join them in an informal setting. Sometimes they succeed as week-night groups, meeting at homes or the church as long as the interest continues. Their virtue is their spontaneity and informality. More often than not, some interested individual inquires about an opportunity for study or suggests it, thereby uncovering a like feeling among others that would otherwise have gone unnoticed.

In one community, a church woman invited four other women to join her in a series of mission study experiences. The following year each of them gathered a group of five women for similar study. The third year the groups had multiplied to twenty-five—all from the original interest and effort of one dedicated woman.

In one small town church, the Sunday morning church school opportunities for adults consist of five interest groups, one of which deals with a mission subject one or two quarters of the year. Church members select the study group that excites their interest most. In another church, a Friendship Press publication provided grist for six sessions of panel and group discussion for Sunday evening services.

THE YOUTH OF THE CHURCH

The youth program of a congregation includes another important opportunity for missionary education beyond the

Sunday morning church school curriculum. Related to one another in the United Christian Youth Movement—the co-operative Protestant youth movement in the United States—many church youth organizations plan their programs in the areas of Christian faith, Christian witness, Christian citizenship, Christian outreach, and Christian fellowship. The youth organizations of churches in Canada co-operate through the Committee on Young People's Work of the Canadian Council of Churches. Aspects of their programs clearly relate to the mission of the church.

The areas of Christian outreach and Christian citizenship are perhaps most readily identified with education for mission, although every area has its mission implications. Christian outreach activities are usually those that help young people know and accept their responsibility in the world-wide mission of the church. The area of interest includes home missions, foreign missions, the ecumenical movement, and interchurch aid or relief and reconstruction. Christian citizenship experiences are those that help young people understand community needs and, on the basis of Christian convictions, work to meet the needs through personal influence and group action. This area embraces service to the local church, service to the community, interracial, interfaith, and intercultural relations, industrial, economic, and social problems, and political education and action.

These purposes and areas of concern represent elements of growth toward maturity for the young person. They clearly show that the Christian youth confronts a large learning task, a very important factor in it being his orientation to the world mission of the church. If he is to grow into mature Christian adulthood, his church must provide him with guidance for growth through action as well as study.

THE CHURCH'S CHILDREN

Interest in missionary work may often begin in early childhood. Many missionaries were born and reared on mission fields by missionary parents. Other children, in mission clubs or through mission books or stories, came early in life to look forward to a missionary vocation for themselves. Such an early impact on a person's life influences him deeply.

In addition to the church school session, extended sessions for children during the hour of church worship, weekday released time classes, and vacation church schools are important opportunities for the missionary education of children. Frequently, Friendship Press publications for children are recommended as official vacation church school texts. In these educational experiences, mission study materials can be used to lead children to a devotion to the Christian mission.

8

Motivating a Church
in Mission

INTEREST IN CHRISTIAN MISSION INDICATES the spiritual health and vigor of a congregation. A strong church is one whose involvement in mission is not lessened when it confronts such problems as supporting a building program, adjusting to a community in transition, or changing leadership. In such situations, a church's commitment to mission is not a burden but a help. Many a church that is newly inspired by its role in mission has found that this inspiration can make the problems of its own congregational life less formidable.

What leads a church to fuller involvement in mission? The real motivation comes from the inner compulsion of the gospel itself. It is the work of God's Spirit among his people, which gives them power and zeal. Yet God uses human instruments to play their part in this process. Those instruments must be responsive.

THE MINISTER'S ROLE

We look to the minister first because of his role as spiritual leader of the congregation. If he is not keenly sensitive to the sweep of Christian mission, his church is likely to flag in zeal. His training and ordination do not automatically ensure that he will possess a missionary outlook. If he himself senses the lack, he can overcome it through reading, travel, conference, or missionary activity. If he seems not to be aware, the tactful suggestions of a concerned layman may be needed.

The missionary education leaders of the congregation can offer their minister a great deal of assistance in enlarging or awakening his mission concern. They may provide him regularly with copies of mission publications or periodicals. They may see that he receives the stimulation of a week at a denominational or interdenominational mission conference. Many a congregation has sent its minister and his wife on an observation trip to mission work overseas or in the homeland. After such an experience, one minister's former coolness to missionary work turned to a deep interest that he pursued through the remainder of his pastoral life, bringing enrichment to himself and giving his church an opportunity to grow in vision and commitment.

The minister needs this mission concern not only for his own spiritual growth but for his adequate ministry to his congregation. He himself must be an agent of motivation to bring others into leadership in this essential aspect of the congregation's life.

AND EVERY LAYMAN

The task is not the minister's alone, however. As in every other phase of church activity, the layman shares the missionary obligation equally with his pastor. We have insisted at several points in this book that missions is not an interest solely of some special group in the church, some special group of missionary zealots. Yet it is usually true in any social organism that there is a specialization of function. Each congregation needs laymen who, because of their sensitivity to the missionary task of the church, will be the leaders, the not-hidden persuaders, the champions of the cause.

The people on whom such responsibility falls must perform their function with Christ-like patience, tact, and winsomeness. They have no cause for pride or excuse for high-handedness in being chosen. Their purpose is to persuade, not repel. Their method is to enlist others, not to manipulate them. The cause of missions could be badly served by well-meaning devotees unable to understand why everyone is not immediately and wholeheartedly as interested as they themselves are. Nevertheless, leaders in education for mission must exhibit vigor and aggressiveness. Their task is a demanding one; it requires perseverance, hard work, and thorough planning.

It is the role, then, of the minister and of the laymen to be the instruments of motivation that lead a congregation to dynamic involvement in mission and to partnership in missions. The task cannot be accomplished overnight. It may take months or even years, for this kind of climate is the outgrowth of an intelligent understanding of the mission. It requires a continuing program of education and experience.

PERSON TO PERSON

No other means of stimulating an interest in the mission of the church equals person to person relationships. Knowledge of the growth of the church should come by firsthand contact, not only through promotional releases or official reports. The telling blow for mission is struck by direct personal relationship with people and places.

Leaders of the younger churches ask for such relationships. Their contacts having been primarily with mission board representatives in the past. Now they seek to be in touch with the church itself in America. They want the sense of direct fellowship, church with church, Christian with Christian. Part of the difficulty in fulfilling their desire is purely administrative, since the churches in North America and Europe have delegated responsibility for missionary work to their mission boards. Nevertheless, this need for Christian fellowship and rapport must be met as fully as possible.

Person to person relationships can occur for North American Christians in either of two ways: They may visit Christians of other communities or countries; or they may receive Christians from other places as guests in their homes and churches. By each means, the Christian fellowship is enlarged and the mission enriched.

MISSIONARY DEPUTATION

The value of personal contact has long been recognized in the use of missionaries on furlough for visits to North American congregations. The desire of congregations for such visits always far outruns the supply, but considerable person to person encounter with the Christian mission is accomplished this way. To do it most efficiently, the denominations usually assign a missionary to a synod or a conference for a period, asking that his time be used to good advantage in the time allotted.

What constitutes effective use of a missionary when he is available to a local church? The church's imagination should lead beyond the request for a speech or two. The talks may be sparkling and colorful, but of even greater value are interchange of ideas, questions, and informal visiting. Small groups, even families, will benefit from conversations with the missionary. The missionary in turn will feel more closely in touch with the life of the church—and less on parade.

Such use of missionaries for deputation has serious difficulties that local church people should understand. After a term of three to five years away from home, the missionary returns tired and worn. One basic purpose of his furlough is rest and change of scene and climate. A heavy itinerary of speaking engagements taxes his already depleted strength. Furthermore, when he has rested or recuperated, he often needs additional training or intellectual refreshment to equip him more adequately for the assignment to which he will be returning. More and more, these workers, chosen because of their high qualifications, find themselves in positions of specialized responsibility that require the enhancing of their skills and information. Too much deputation detracts from this necessary professional improvement.

Missionaries find themselves in a dilemma when they do deputation work. The inviting church wants to hear something encouraging and exciting; this is to be an occasion of stimulation for the congregation. A missionary's integrity requires that he also reflect the problems, the failures, the perplexities of the mission. To share in these concerns is most healthful for a Christian congregation, but it is the sort of thing done best in informal discussion and not from the pulpit or in platform addresses.

Visits between missionaries and fraternal workers and members of local congregations are valuable and desirable. Each denomination gives guidance in this matter; that guidance should be followed sympathetically and imaginatively. Occasions of missionary visits benefit both congregation and missionary.

FRATERNAL FELLOWSHIP

The visits of Christians from other parts of the world provide another opportunity for person to person relationship. Such visitors obviously will be even fewer than missionaries. Their time, therefore, must be used still more carefully. Because they are in a strange community or culture, all the more care must be exercised in order that communication with them be an honest, mutual experience. Let us never be guilty of exploiting visitors for our own purposes.

One who has traveled in a number of countries comes to know how welcome the sincere hospitality of strangers can be. That pleasant little surprise by which your host reminds you of home. Those gracious introductions to the customs of his own land. That sure knowledge of openhearted welcome of you just as you are. Such are the touches that should grace our reception of Christian friends from other parts of our nation or world. Fawning praise, prying curiosity, or overweening hospitality are embarrassing. Brash display or domineering boastfulness are offensive. Let us be ourselves to our visitors—that is, our best selves. It is mutuality of interest and concern in these visits with other Christians that will bring the most creative results.

Overseas students, pursuing higher education in the colleges and universities of our continent, provide us with our easiest access to fellowship with persons of other places and cultures. In 1960, there were forty thousand such students from many countries. Few American communities are too remote to be unable to get in touch with several such young men and women, if they would. Many are scholarship students, brought under the sponsorship of the denominations. Information about them can be secured at denominational headquarters. Many others can be reached through the Committee on Friendly Relations with Foreign Students, an agency that welcomes them on their arrival and keeps in touch with them during and after their student years. Most colleges and universities will provide help in establishing such contacts through their registrar's or chaplain's office or through a special counselor for overseas students.

Many of these guests are not Christians. They may be devout Hindus, Muslims, Buddhists, or they may be purely secular in outlook. Non-Christian students often are the forgotten ones, returning to their homelands without visiting very many—if any—Christian homes of North America. They have much to teach us, and we should include them in our invitations. We should be respectful of their religion and of their culture. In some instances, we may learn to know them well enough so that religious discussion could be constructive. In the first instance, however, our Christian witness should be in our friendly hospitality, our loving interest, our example. The purpose of the visits is not conversion; it is fellowship and understanding.

Even in entertaining Christian students, we must be careful about exploiting them for our interests, overindulging them with gifts or attention, offending them with thoughtless curiosity. Here is an opportunity for creative Christian fellowship across boundaries of space and culture that too widely separate us from our Christian brothers. Hosts to overseas students should be instructed and given guidance so that they know how to converse thoughtfully with these young guests, avoiding paternalistic or patronizing attitudes toward them. The opportunity provided by their visits merits thoughtful use.

One denomination has experimented by placing some

overseas students in churches as staff members, assisting with parish calling and group meetings. They became members of the leadership teams of the churches, not mission exhibits. The relationship made a real mission impact and was a start in making missions a "two-way street."

If this discussion seems to be entirely about persons from Afghanistan or Africa, Europe or Uruguay, it is at fault. We need to remember that there are also boundaries that limit our fellowship with brothers nearer at home—farmer, Indian, apartment dweller, Negro, white, and recent immigrant. Understanding any of these persons increases from person to person contacts. Refugees settled in North American communities and received into the Christian fellowship of the church help build a bridge across still another boundary. The Christian mission calls us to concern for the needs of one another. Many local churches have carried on creative meetings across boundaries and in doing so have enlarged their sense of mission and their bonds of brotherhood.

THE MERITS OF TRAVEL

Personal contacts are a two-way street. Improved facilities at economical rates and increasing leisure make travel easier than ever before. Many North American church members are discovering the thrill of giving their travel a new dimension by visiting people and places in which they have a mission concern.

One denomination plans several traveling seminars to various parts of the United States each year. One of these seminar groups tours Indian reservations and institutions of the West and Southwest to acquaint the participants with the Christian work there. Another makes a similar trip to Puerto Rico or Cuba. Still another may go to Alaska or Hawaii, or may visit the home mission institutions of the nation's large cities.

Another denomination conducts an overseas tour each year, selecting the part of the world in which that year's world mission study theme is placed. One year it was the Middle East, another it was Africa. What else could it have been in a year when the theme was "Into All the World Together" than a round-the-world trip!

Many laymen who enrolled for these tours just for the excursion have ended up enthusiastic champions of the church's mission. Some few who were in professions like medicine or engineering have offered themselves for short term service when they saw a need their skills could serve.

On a smaller scale, many local churches are sponsoring group trips to mission institutions, migrant camps, settlement houses, or other home mission projects. A chartered bus transports the group, if they do not travel by auto caravan, sometimes visiting places of historic or scenic interest on the way. A young Pennsylvania woman, after several years of voluntary summer service among Spanish Americans in New Mexico, has conducted annual bus tours to that area for groups of church members from her home.

Many Christian laymen work overseas in the employ of government agencies or private businesses. Many others are stationed at armed forces installations around the world.

These persons, too, are in positions for valuable face to face contacts with Christians of other lands. Before beginning their tours of duty, they should learn about the people and churches where they will live and work. While there, they should contact the congregations, joining them in Christian fellowship and assisting them in their work whenever possible.

For young people, similar experiences come through caravans and work camps. In one program, small groups of Christian youth, carefully chosen for caravan duty, receive thorough training for the work. They then travel from place to place, stopping a week or two at a number of previously arranged locations. Sometimes they direct vacation church schools, train local youth for better Christian youth work, paint or repair small churches, or perform other needed service. Work camps more frequently locate for a period of weeks or months in one place, where the work of hands and minds can meet an evident pressing need. The work camp experience usually involves college or older youth, often in interracial and international teams. They have built playgrounds, created retreat facilities, erected chapels, helped clear away slums. Sometimes, as at Agapé in Italy, a Christian retreat center, the project continues summer after summer until the completion of an extensive task in which various groups have had a part. All the while, both in caravans and in work camps, young people have worked shoulder to shoulder with the people of the community they have served, joining them in study and worship.

Other experiences, such as student exchange programs and student conferences, also provide an ecumenical fellowship in Christian mission.

This has been a brief introduction to the several kinds of face to face encounter with Christian missions. A congregation will do well to investigate these opportunities and to participate in them. No other means of motivation will be so productive.

PARTNERSHIP IN SHARING

Although financial participation in a particular mission project stimulates missionary concern, a church's giving cannot always be direct. Denominational mission boards encourage churches to contribute to their general budgets. The reason is clear: denominational headquarters must have the freedom and the resources to distribute help where and when it is needed. To leave this responsibility to the whims and fancies of local groups of Christians would create chaos in the total missionary endeavor.

Yet congregations want to feel related to the persons or institutions their contributions are assisting. Most denominations make provision for this kind of giving, over and above the support they ask for the basic budget. Such opportunities for giving may involve entering a relationship of missionary partners, associated congregations, or fraternal associations. When a congregation establishes this sort of channel, it finds a delight in its mission activity that a purely impersonal relationship cannot supply.

A missionary, thus supported, writes: "This church pays

my salary, but it does far more than that—it upholds my
hands, it inspires me to more faithful service, and it makes
my heart rejoice by its love and devotion to its missionary.
And if I am successful in the work for which I have been
sent to Iran, it will be largely because I am not alone, but
hundreds of members of Calvin Church are working with
me."

Direct relationships lift missionary interest beyond the
level of financial support alone. Minister and congregational
leaders can strengthen them in a number of ways by reading correspondence from the missionary or the associated
church, by frequent references in sermon or prayer, and
by recognition of the relationship in church publications.

Money is simply a means of exchange, a substitute for
barter or reciprocal service. Used in Christian causes, it
is a sacramental instrument. It expresses by its tangible
power the love, the good will, the service, the prayers, the
fellowship of one Christian for another. Many congregations give as much money for work beyond their own local
program as they do to support the program itself. In this
way, they demonstrate their dedication to the mission of
the church.

In most denominations, special giving projects and goals
for young people enlist their support of mission work.
Through World Youth Projects, Christian youth in many
countries share with one another, creating an ecumenical
fellowship through their giving. The projects to which
their gifts are sent include, for example, youth camps in
Thailand, an interracial retreat in South Africa, and leader-

ship training in such countries as India, the Philippines, Korea, and Brazil.

Children, too, participate in giving projects. When such projects help them feel a direct relationship with children of other lands, they are creative and educational experiences. Two familiar, popular projects have been *Pictures for Children Everywhere* and *Stories of Jesus for Children Everywhere,* sponsored by the World Council of Christian Education. Gifts of children in Canada and the United States have made attractive pictures and stories available to thousands of children around the world, thereby improving their Christian instruction.

As we have seen, we need to think of a missionary offering as an expression of serious missionary concern, not merely as a means of raising money. Stewardship and missions are inextricably intertwined. They spring from the same gospel roots.

A MISSIONARY STEWARDSHIP

Thinking of stewardship in missions, we need to be aware of a difficult and subtle problem for the sincere Christian. A familiar adage says that the way to lose a friend is to lend him money. Like many proverbs, it is only half true. Yet there is something of the same risk in making other people the constant recipients of our generosity. Benevolence overdone can impoverish, humiliate, or embarrass the very people we want to help. Given condescendingly, money can curse rather than bless. Any tendency for us to be proud of our generosity may lead to a blighting

of the gifts and the Christian service they are intended to
accomplish.

The solution is by no means to stop giving. We who are
blessed with abundance must learn to share it with humil-
ity, tact, and sincere love. It then becomes sacramental, to
be used by the Holy Spirit to establish Christian fellowship and to meet human need.

Missionary giving must have as its goal the ultimate self-
sufficiency of the recipient. Anything that hinders attain-
ing this goal is detrimental and impoverishing. Any attempt to establish a kind of work that the receiving church
itself cannot hope to support in the future must be suspect.
Giving is a fine art, and education for mission should help
each of us recognize those aspects of the art that need
further development in his own life.

It deserves repeating here that missionary giving is not
an activity in which the West only sends and the rest of
the world only receives. We who can provide money and
personnel are not without our own needs, needs that can
be met only with the help of other Christians.

Here our home missions situation is instructive. The
wealthy city church gives help to a remote rural church,
and a shortsighted view would be that mission assistance
is just going in one direction. Yet for a long while, it has
been recognized that city churches have not provided their
own recruits for the ministry; these have often come from
the smaller, less affluent rural churches. The mission is a
reciprocal relationship. We need one another for those particular gifts with which God has endowed us. The giver of

money may well need to be the recipient of insight or understanding.

CELEBRATING THE MISSION

Special occasions of a festive nature often stimulate an interest in the mission of the church, occasionally in connection with an effort to meet a financial goal. A church in Wisconsin set a goal of one thousand dollars for the Christian World Mission and began to plan months ahead for a Thank Offering Dinner in November. Every church group and organization was informed of the plans and invited to participate in gathering the offering and in arranging the all-church event. The ten women's guilds were each assigned two tables to decorate and the girls of the youth fellowship were enlisted as waitresses. The church members were assigned to tables, with a couple at each table serving as hosts.

The program consisted of a Thanksgiving litany, the dedication of the Thank Offering, and an address on the Christian World Mission. Grain, bread, and blossoms were presented along with the Thank Offering at the altar that had been set up in the center of the banquet hall. The dedication ceremony expressed gratitude to God for his goodness and set apart the offering to the work of Christ's kingdom in the world. When the total of the money offering was announced, the people responded, "We did more than we thought we could."

In some districts or synods, churches are joining to plan and carry out mission festivals; their purpose is to inspire as large a number of people as possible with the Christian mission. The festivals are usually one-day occurrences, often on a Sunday afternoon and evening, and are widely publicized.

A typical program consists of a variety of unusual features. In a large room of the host church, booths are set up, decorated, and outfitted with materials from different countries and continents. They contain curios, pictures, books, periodicals—anything to enhance interest in that part of the world. Conversation corners are arranged where people may stop for an informal chat with visiting missionaries, Christian nationals, or other church leaders with experience in the missionary work of the church. Films are shown continuously in a projection room where visitors may stop for as long as they choose. A workshop for leaders of missionary education is arranged for a certain hour and announced in advance of the festival. After an opportunity for sack lunches or refreshments, an evening program brings the whole group together for worship. Combined choirs of the participating congregations provide the music. An outstanding speaker delivers the missionary challenge.

A well-planned festival makes a great impact. More people can be reached than with most other types of program. It demonstrates the fact that the mission is something to be shared, something of interest to large audiences. It can result in the organizing of missionary education activities in local churches where there was none before. It often will be followed spontaneously by local festivals. It is not a substitute for serious study, but it is a popular way to interest large numbers of people in missions.

A Long Island church planned something of this sort for itself, calling it a World-Church Week End. The Friday evening dinner presented an international menu, followed by an address on the Christian mission. Saturday was open house day, with scheduled exhibits, film presentations, children's program, and mission seminars. On Sunday morning the program was climaxed by a sermon preached by a noted educator from Taiwan.

Examples and variations are too numerous to cite. A church with a missionary interest will take unusual delight in this sort of activity. One where the interest lags may find it a stimulant for its own awakening.

ON EXHIBIT

Exhibits may by themselves be a means of education for mission. They may be placed in the church vestibule or in its social room where from week to week people, as they come and go, will be reminded of some aspect of the work of the church around the world. A large map of the world offers itself for such use. So do enlarged pictures and posters. A church in Harrisburg, Pa., while studying Africa, had a child-sized thatched hut, surrounded by other attractive symbols of African life, in its foyer. At the other side of the foyer, there was a complete display of publications about Africa that people could examine and buy.

Some churches have permanent displays, to remind members of their partnership in mission with churches in all the world. A church in Berkeley, Calif., has created a World Mission Room, equipped with maps and pictures to keep the congregation conscious of its outreach in service and fellowship. Such a room is used constantly by church organizations; it is not a museum.

A CAUSE FOR PRAYER

When all is said and done, nothing will have a more abiding or far-reaching effect in creating a climate for mission than the prayer life of the congregation. Christ emphasized this important duty when he commanded: ". . . Pray therefore the Lord of the harvest to send out laborers into his harvest." (Luke 10:2.) Dr. J. Christie Wilson of Princeton Theological Seminary has suggested that a church's missionary interests be supported by:

1. Prayer for the preaching of the gospel, for ambassadors of the cross, for the churches in mission lands, for those who suffer persecution for Christ; and that the church here may be filled with vision and give with liberality and self-sacrifice.

2. Prayer for specific missionaries from the church or supported by the church, for missionaries and projects supported by church organizations.

3. Missionary praying in all services and all departments of the church, suggesting special objects and persons for individual prayer.

4. Use of the mission prayer guide provided by the denomination.

5. Prayer meetings for missionary intercession.

6. Prayer for the benevolence giving.

7. Prayer for the consecration of life.

The last point suggests what may be one of the best clues to the missionary climate of a congregation. Has it sent out from its midst young men and women who are dedicated to church vocations at home or in other parts of the world? Are lives being consecrated to the mission of the church? To be sure, this is a part of the mysterious working of the Holy Spirit, but he works where doors are open and people sensitive to his will. Young people need to be encouraged in their homes and inspired by their churches to consider a church vocation as their life's calling.

9

Creative Leadership

EDUCATION FOR MISSION DEALS WITH SOME of the most exciting and crucial issues of our day. It is concerned with the dynamic movements of Christian faith and action in a turbulent world. It comprehends the crises of mankind—hunger, disease, loneliness, meaninglessness, and strife. It tells of the meeting of human needs in a way that has universal, eternal meaning.

When education for mission lacks good leadership, when it fails to employ vital methods of discovery and learning, it is dull, ineffective, irrelevant. To be effective, missionary education calls for training, planning, imagination, and dedication.

AGE-GROUP GRADING

Let us begin with the matter of grading. Graded experiences of learning are as important in education for mission as they are in any other form of education. In general, it is agreed that the educational experiences of the church be organized into children's, youth, and adult divisions. The children are separated into nursery, 2 to 3 years old; kindergarten, 4 to 5 years old; primary, 6 to 8 years old or grades 1 to 3; and junior, 9 to 11 years old or grades 4 to 6. The youth division comprises junior high, 12 to 14 years old or grades 7 to 9; senior high, 15 to 17 years old or grades 10 to 12, and older youth, 18 to 24 years old. This latter age range cannot be held rigidly, since many young people are married before they are twenty-four years old, and married couples should be grouped with the young adults. At this age and through adulthood, groups should be formed more with respect to mutual interests and needs than to age. Adults may be classed as young adults, ages 25 to 34 years; middle adults, ages 35 to 65 years; and older adults, beyond 65 years.

The education for mission accomplished in the Sunday church school will already have the benefit of this grading, in so far as the size of the church permits thorough organization. Other special missionary education opportunities, such as the school of missions or the church family night, will be more effective if parts of their program are arranged by age-group interests and abilities.

Grading implies that there are leaders for each age-group who understand the needs of the particular age-group and the methods by which learning and growth can most creatively be achieved. Many materials are available for the guidance of these leaders in the general field of education and in the more particular field of Christian education. We are concerned here only with a few considerations that relate these principles more precisely to learning about the Christian mission.

MISSIONARY EDUCATION OF CHILDREN

What is missionary education of children? In the earliest years of a child's life, Christian education lays a foundation for later education for mission. Small children have not yet developed the capacity for judgment and abstract concepts. Limits of time and space have not taken on much significance for them. They know most clearly the present moment and the persons with whom they live and play. Concepts of mission and missionary work in distant places are beyond them.

One of the fundamental goals of education for mission is that persons should develop respect and love for all people as persons for whom Christ died. Thus we begin with small children in helping them to develop love and appreciation for other boys and girls, even for their toys and for the animals with which they play. Through his parents and teachers, a child comes to know love and to understand something of God's love for him in Christ. The child learns that children in all parts of the world live in homes with their parents, receive care and affection, and enjoy their pets and toys too. He learns that God loves all children in the world with a love made known in Jesus Christ. In response, the child comes to feel love for all people everywhere.

As the child's experience progresses, his circle of interest and understanding expands. He begins in his late primary years to notice more specifically the differences between people. Even then, he is made aware of the differences more by the adult world than by his own consciousness of them. Education for mission has the task of helping him to understand these differences of skin color, language, accent, customs, and temperament, and to accept them as being only surface differences under which lies the same human unity that he took for granted as a smaller child. The growth of prejudice may be thwarted here by wholesome experiences of fellowship with children of other backgrounds, either directly where possible or vicariously through story and drama.

The junior child has begun to use his imagination still more widely. The elements of time and space begin to have more meaning for him, particularly if he has the good fortune of traveling with his family or of reading with them about distant places and people. His curiosity now has wider and deeper interests, raising questions about life that require answers. "Why did God make people to speak different languages?" "Why are their houses in other lands different from ours?" "Do other people have churches like our beautiful one on the corner?"

Education for mission has the task, not only of awakening in the child an interest in people in all parts of the world and a feeling of regard for them, but also of answering questions about them and of relating the life and love of Jesus Christ to them all. The smart-as-a-whip junior boy or girl, alertly watching his world expand through experiences at school or through reading or television, begins to be aware that the church he attends week by week has counterparts elsewhere in his community, in his nation, and around the world.

For children, the attitudes, moods, and behavior of their parents and leaders are of utmost importance. Children are imitators by nature, consciously and unconsciously. They learn more from what we are and do in their presence than from what we say. The leader's spirit of love, enthusiasm, and devotion for the church say more about the mission of the church than his words. In this, parents and teachers together provide the foundation for further growth in the child's character.

Methods for the missionary education of children vary with the ages of the children and with their previous experiences and present needs. These methods are admirably presented in Edith Welker's *Friends With All the World,* a Friendship Press manual for children's workers. This book, together with supplementary resources such as *Here's How and When,* by Armilda B. Keiser; *Let's Play a Story,* by Elizabeth Allstrom; and *Missionary Stories to Play and Tell,* by Nina Millen, are indispensable tools for the missionary education of children.

MISSIONARY EDUCATION OF YOUTH

For young people, education for mission offers wide opportunities for exploration and understanding. The junior high is an adolescent. He is becoming a more self-conscious individual. He has his own problems of adjustment to family and society; in them he feels the need for the security of his peer group. He understands loneliness, joy, purposefulness, achievement. At his stage of growth, he is learning to identify himself with others, understanding their hopes¹ and fears and putting himself in their place with unselfish interest. In searching for maturity for himself, he idealizes his hopes in the lives of certain persons who have achieved success in their own fields—a home run champ, this year's popular singer, a space age physicist. His heroes could also be a missionary or a Christian leader in India.

The vicarious security and achievement that the adolescent finds in those who have done notable things make biography interesting to him. The adventures of the Christian mission on our national frontiers or in distant places convey to him a sense of the challenge of that mission.

He also has his questions about the church, a curiosity more sophisticated than that of his younger brother or sister. He wants to know a great deal more about people, how they live, what they do, what they think and feel. Stories still have their appeal and value, for they convey information with the warmth and impact that attract the whole person of the adolescent.

The older brother or sister, involved in the complex high school or college world, has still more sophisticated interests. The arena of the mind is challenging him, although he is often childish in his enthusiasm for play or pranks. His science teachers, by introducing him to laws of nature and theories of the universe's origin, have brought him face to face with some problems of faith. He has had a look at history and international affairs. How does the missionary work of the church fit into the picture of the world that is forming in his mind? Is it right for Christians to desire all other people to be converted to their faith?

Education for mission now inherits the task of answering many searching questions. As the youth grows older, stories about the mission no longer fully satisfy. His mind raises issues; he becomes a philosopher of sorts. He must have a chance to try out new ideas, to gnaw at persistent doubts, to work out a position that his mind as well as his heart can respect. He will not easily accept the dictum of the adult leader in church; he wants a friend who is flexible enough to consider some of his own ideas with him.

To the process of education for mission, the growing youth brings many assets. His knowledge of the world has expanded; his familiarity with world affairs has broadened. He has advanced in his faith and in his active participation in the church. He has probably become a communicant of his church. All this helps him to understand not only the material aspects of the Christian mission in the world but its spiritual purposes, its wholeness. He is growing toward maturity in his faith and practice as a Christian. He must now explore more deeply the biblical foundations for Christian mission and the theological ground for his own responsibility in mission.

Methods for accomplishing the missionary education of youth are dealt with fully in two books. In *Wide as the World,* Louise Griffiths has carefully described the principles to be followed, values to be achieved, and projects to be developed in working with junior high or intermediate youth. D. Campbell Wyckoff's *In One Spirit* presents the philosophy of the Christian mission and methods for helping senior high youth understand its activity in the world. These two Friendship Press texts, together with many other supplementary resources, are essential for leaders of youth.

MISSIONARY EDUCATION OF ADULTS

What can be said about educating adults for the mission of the church? Here the whole gamut of experience and growth opens up before the leader. The only limitations are those of the particular group of adults with whom he may be working, their previous training and development, their needs and interests, their position in the Christian fellowship. To lead these adults into fuller maturity will challenge the best in any leader.

While the missionary education of adults presents an unlimited opportunity, there is a relatively small amount of creative adult education and too few adults are involved in it. For one reason, many adults feel their lives are already overcrowded with obligations and interests. For another, many have never been attracted to a program of missionary education of real consequence for them. The secret is to bring need and interest together.

For the young adults, the secret often is their young families. Parents of growing children soon discover how much they need to know in order to guide their children's growth properly. The unmarried young adult may develop his interest in the Christian mission through travel or occupation. In middle age, adults are fully involved in the issues with which their world confronts them—livelihood, civic well-being, peace, for example. Intelligent participation in the world mission of the church fills out the picture. Older adults, exploring new fields of interest and activity after relinquishing some of the responsibilities they have carried most of their adult lives, can find in the Christian mission a most intriguing exploration. All, purely because of their Christian commitment, will find in missions their faith's fullest expression.

INFORMALITY IN ADULT EDUCATION

If one basic rule were to be given for improving adult education, it would be to increase the informality of the process and group participation in it. Dr. Thomas Gordon in "How to Lead Discussions" writes: "Too often we think of communication as simply that which is expressed by someone. Communication, however, requires that an expression make an impression on the listener. We cannot assume always that the meaning of the expression will be identical to the meaning of the impression. Consequently, effective communication between people occurs only when

$$Expression = Impression.$$

In other words, real understanding of the meaning of a speaker occurs only when the listener's impression is exactly what the speaker intended it to be."[1]

[1] Gordon, Thomas. "Planning for Discussion," *How to Lead Discussions*. Chicago: Adult Education Association of the U.S.A., 1955, p. 20.

The discussion group method is one that, with variations, will serve most effectively in securing participation and expression. People will remember far longer what they talked about than what they heard. Furthermore, they will have had a chance to raise questions, test their judgments against those of others, disagree when moved to, and clarify their understanding of the subject.

Dr. Gordon suggests the following helpful outline for the leader's preparation:

1. You might try out techniques for getting members to participate *before* the first meeting.
   Send out questionnaires to get information about:
   > *Members' interests*
   > *Real problems they are facing*
   > *Questions on their minds*

   Ask a few members if they would serve on a Planning Committee which might work out a tentative program for the *first* meeting.

2. You might gather the best resources you can find for use *by the group*. Your attitude would be: What can I make available to the group as possible resources for the members to choose?
   > Appropriate moving pictures
   > Case studies
   > Recordings
   > Book Lists (selected carefully for pertinence)
   > Situations suitable for role-playing
   > Possible field trips

3. You might get your own ideas organized in suitable form for use by the group, if the members decide to use you as one of their resources. You need not fear being prepared as well as you can be, just don't let your preparation divert the group.

4. You might want to take steps to insure that the physical resources for the group will be conducive to effective discussion.

If your group will be large, you might arrange to reserve several smaller rooms for sub-group discussion, in case the group decides to subdivide.

Try to get comfortable rooms in which the chairs can be moved into a circle or square.

Remove all symbols of leadership, such as podiums, platforms, gavels, special chairmen's chairs, teachers' desks, lecterns.

You might bring materials which can be used as name tags.

5. You might feel more comfortable if you planned what you will say to the group at the opening of the first meeting, keeping in mind that:

The more you say the more you encourage the members to depend on you to carry the ball alone.

Any hint you give about how they should get started will be only too welcome. So you may not get ideas from the group unless you *avoid having preconceptions* about where they should begin.

If you *do* think you know where the group should begin, plan your opening remarks to give the members a chance to make suggestions *before you make yours*. Their ideas may be better than yours.[2]

THE LEADER OF GROUP DISCUSSION

These principles may seem to apply to an informal, problem-solving group more than to a mission study group. Nevertheless, careful consideration of them will transform the leadership skills of many a person. Dr. T. H. P. Sailer, dean of missionary education in the United States, suggests

[2] *Ibid.*, p. 15.

a missionary discussion group leader ought to have these qualities:

1. Deep interest in your subject and contagious enthusiasm for it. You cannot give what you do not have. If you are a bromide, you will put others to sleep. Keep a notebook and fill it with ideas.

2. Interest in what others think. Therefore, don't be a soloist and talk all the time, even if you are the best talker and know more than the others. What counts is not what you give out but what they take in and what they are likely to do with it when they get it.

3. Ability to draw people out. This is not only to help you learn about them, but to help them to make up their minds. This last they will do best by expressing themselves. Stimulating this is the hardest part of leading a discussion.

4. Ability to profit by experience. You cannot be blamed for making mistakes, but only for making the same mistake twice. After every session review your work as if you were a critic or teacher. Try to discover why things went wrong and to think what you should have done.

5. Time to prepare. You can make time for what you consider supremely important. If you do not believe that leading a discussion group is sufficiently important to find time for careful preparation, it is safe to say that the Lord has not called you to this work.

PRESENTATIONS UNDERGIRD DISCUSSION

Does this emphasis on informal group discussion imply that other forms of education are not valid, that there is no place for an address, presentation, book review, or film? By no means. Presentation of information, however, has much greater success when it is a resource for group consideration than when it is expected to stand on its own feet alone. Discussion of course may be only "the pooling of ignorance," as critics of group processes declare, if it is not given perceptive leadership and if it is not fed from a reservoir of authoritative information.

Where can such information be found? The easiest and perhaps most frequently used source is the informed speaker—perhaps the minister, or a missionary, or a student of the issue. Sometimes the role must be performed by the teacher or leader of the group, who prepares himself thoroughly by extensive study. This is a valuable means of presentation for it transmits information to the accompaniment of the speaker's emotional overtones.

A book may be the resource. It will best serve this purpose if the members of the group have all read it in advance. They will then be prepared to discuss it and to explore other areas of information suggested to them by the message of the book. Or the book may be reviewed by one of the group. This takes talent and careful preparation if the review is not to be dry as dust or superficially meager in its communication.

An excellent resource for presentation is the motion picture or the filmstrip, carefully selected for its treatment of the subject to be discussed. These tools combine visual images with verbal ones, and they add the emotional impact of dramatized real-life situations. Except in a few instances in which the audio-visual is designed for worship or meditation, the showing ought to be followed by discussion. Do not follow the lazy habit of relying on a film to provide a program for you.

Films and filmstrips are usually produced interdenominationally or by the denominations on the annual mission study themes. These will be your best audio-visual resources when studying those themes, though there are abundant materials, both religious and secular, which can be found to have an illuminating bearing on the study.

Panel discussions or symposiums provide another method for getting facts before a group, so it may get its teeth into the meaty aspects of the subject. The panel discussion is composed of four or five persons who have done advance preparation so they can debate the main issues of the study, stimulating the whole group to get into the act. A symposium usually gives three or four persons an opportunity to make separate, consecutive talks on several aspects of the subject before the group discusses these questions. In either of these cases, care is necessary so the presentations do not exhaust the subject or the listeners. They are intended to be provocative and stimulating, not exhaustive or exhausting.

In role playing, a relatively new educational technique, persons spontaneously act out problems of human relations and analyze the enactment with the help of the observers. It is widely recognized as a method of helping people to broaden their understanding of other people, to see things from the point of view of the person on the other side of the table, the tracks, or the globe. This makes it a useful technique in missionary education, when employed sparingly, intelligently, and with careful planning.

The greatest advantage with this method is achieved when the role play is discussed after it has been done. The director should carefully brief each participant about his role, introduce the setting, and end the presentation when it has gone on long enough to stimulate discussion—but before it has worn itself out. He should then direct the group in evaluating the attitudes and emotions that were expressed. The scene might be played a second time with new understanding after the group discussion.

Informal dramatization or impersonation is an interesting method. Dr. Sailer relates the technique to missionary discussion group activity, recommending that it be organized well in advance in order to be effective. "Some of the most vital problems in missionary work are due to conflicting interests of different groups on the field. One of the most acute of these is between black and white in South Africa. In other sections there are clashes between landlords and peasants, upper and lower classes of society, radicals and conservatives, which greatly affect missionary efforts. Such situations may be made more impressive by imaginary interviews of persons representing different viewpoints. These must be based on fairly accurate knowledge and presented with deep seriousness."

A more familiar method of dramatic presentation is the one-act play or the dramatic discussion starter. These prepared materials may either be rehearsed so the participants can act out their parts without use of the script or they may be read. Their purpose again is to provide background for further discussion and exploration. Their advantage is that they combine emotional impact with factual information and involve observers as well as participants.

DIAGNOSING THE PROCESS

These activities represent only a few of the methods of presentation on which group discussion may be solidly based. After the discussion, the leader will know how to improve the group processes if he learns to utilize what the experts in group activity call "feed-back." This is actually a diagnosis of what has happened in the group. In formal classroom situations it is often an examination. In informal groups, even the behavior of the group itself during the meeting is a clue to its response—sleepiness, apathy, alertness, excited discussion. The leader may go further and have private conferences with members of the group after the meeting to find out how they felt about the meeting. Members of the group may list questions they would like to pursue further. Not all the questions should be answered in one session; some should be stored up for later sessions. Evaluation sheets on which the leader has written leading questions may be used to discover what members of the group liked or disliked about the meeting. When the members have a chance to talk back, confident that what they have to say will make a difference, their participation increases.

HELP FOR THE LEADER

Many may rebel, saying, "This is hardly for me. Where can I ever get enough training to be this sort of leader?"

Fortunately there are many sources of help. One of the first to look for is the leader's guide that usually accompanys a missionary education course for children, youth, or adults. The guides suggest more helps than most leaders can use and include practical suggestions for group discussion and action. In addition, there are basic texts for missionary education leaders that have already been mentioned: *Friends With All the World,* by Kelsey; *Here's How and When,* by Keiser; *Wide As the World,* by Griffiths; *In One Spirit,* by Wyckoff. Each of these deals in more detail with the particular age-group involved.

Leadership education help is also available in many churches and communities. Workers conferences for church school leaders might occasionally be devoted to missionary education needs, particularly prior to certain special efforts in the church. Community leadership training schools or institutes can provide help, either in the general age-group classes for leaders and teachers or in one of several specific courses in the Standard Leadership Curriculum that deal with education for mission. These courses are:

150a and b	Missionary Education in the Local Church
151a	At Work for a Christian World
151b	The Christian World Mission
152a and b	The Christian Task at Home
153a and b	The Christian Task Abroad
214b	Missionary Education of Children
315.15b	Youth and the World-Wide Mission of the Church[3]

[3] See *Leadership Education Curriculum Handbook,* 1959-60 Edition, Division of Christian Education, NCCCUSA.

In many communities, the council of churches or the council of church women sponsors an institute or workshops on the annual mission study themes and on basic purposes of missionary education. They deal not only with the interpretation of the study themes, but with methods and materials for their presentation. These are opportunities that local leaders have readily at hand and ought not miss.

Beyond the local community, there are many institutes and conferences on the Christian mission and missionary education. Some are denominationally sponsored; others are interdenominational in character. They are held in synods, annual conferences, dioceses, regions, and jurisdictions. Any leader who has not heard of one of these opportunities has only to ask his minister or inquire from his denominational headquarters and he can be given ample information. Eight or nine of the interdenominational conferences, sponsored by the National Council of Churches, are placed in regions covering the United States and parts of Canada, providing a kind of post-graduate experience in Christian mission and putting it into an ecumenical setting.

10

Tools and Resources

MORE RESOURCES LIE NEAR AT HAND FOR education for mission than most persons have eyes to see. A little grubbing, a little prospecting turn up the treasure.

What are the needs? A speaker, perhaps. Or illustrative information. Audio-visual materials to enrich the program? Pictures and decorative supplies for a banquet or exhibit? Current facts to tie education for mission to contemporary events?

It is impossible to foresee every need, but we can acquaint ourselves with people and places whose services cover a vast range of interests and activities that are relevant to our concern.

PERSONS AND POSSESSIONS

In each church and community, for example, there are more people who could be of help than might be imagined. Many qualify as a result of one kind of travel or another.

Some have been away recently on business trips; their personal contact with people and places may give firsthand information for a mission study program. Some have been overseas in the armed forces or in other types of government service. Still others have vacationed in fascinating places. Their kodachromes, their souvenirs, or an account of their adventures could strengthen a presentation on the part of the world they have visited.

Humans, like squirrels, are hoarders and collectors. The variety of collections possessed by friends in church or community would be surprising. Stamps, picture post cards, china, coins, books—one never knows what kind of collection will turn up next. Some of them can be related to mission study, stimulating imagination and adding colorful side lights.

Persons with certain useful cultivated interests may also be discovered. Some may have specialized in collecting biographies of Livingstone, for instance. Others may have developed a special knowledge of the history of one country or another. Some men and women have business connections that bring them in touch with the products or people of an area of study. A little inquiry, a good memory, and trained observation will turn up surprising program assets in the middle of any circle of acquaintances.

THE CHURCH LIBRARY

Some churches have a well-equipped library. Where there is none, the missionary education leaders may be the persons to see that one is started. Guidance for establishing and maintaining a church library is given in the pamphlet, *Your Church Library*.[1] The collection should include a Bible dictionary, commentaries on the Bible, missionary biographies, publications on various aspects of the missionary enterprise at home and abroad, mission study books from previous years, and stories to illuminate missionary programs. The library should have at least a collection of pictures or filmstrips for audio-visual needs. When the annual mission study materials for a year have served their purpose, they should be placed in the library for later supplementary use with other themes as well as for general reading.

In addition to a church's library, its minister maintains a useful collection of books and resources. His shelves are likely to be especially rich in Bible commentaries, worship resources, and books that deal with the theological foundations of the Christian mission. He needs them for his own preparation, so they should be used sparingly and returned promptly. Yet he will certainly help willingly with what he has, or assist in finding materials from other sources he may know.

COMMUNITY FACILITIES

Most communities have a number of agencies whose facilities are available for use. One of the first is the council of churches. The council's staff and facilities exist to serve the churches; education for mission is one of the co-opera-

[1] Published by the Division of Christian Education, National Council of Churches.

tive activities ready-made for council service. The council should own a display of the missionary education materials for the current year's studies. A special offer of these materials is made to each council of churches. The council should conduct an institute or training program for the development of local leaders and it can aid in finding competent speakers and leaders for special programs. The council may be the depository for audio-visual equipment and materials at a reasonable cost.

The local council of church women also offers valuable assistance. Its observance of special days such as World Day of Prayer and May Fellowship Day, and its encouragement of World Wide Communion Sunday and of the One Great Hour of Sharing, will support a local church's missionary activity. Its institutes and leadership development programs strengthen leaders for their local tasks and give solidarity to the Christian witness in the community.

Public libraries gladly serve local church needs when they are aware of them. Their shelves contain biographies, histories, and general publications whose information can be employed usefully. The librarian may offer to prepare a special resource shelf or exhibit relating to the theme of study, especially when it is known that several of the churches of the community will be pursuing the study at approximately the same time. The library may also be a depository for pictures, kodachromes, maps, or filmstrips. Publications describing private or government projects in the part of the world in which a mission study is concentrating should not be overlooked. Those activities will throw a new light on the needs and opportunities for Christian service.

For local color and decorative interest, a neighboring travel agency may be helpful. It is interested in distributing attractive information about places that tourists might like to see. It may lend large display posters to brighten an exhibit or banquet, and brochures to describe places and people in different detail than the mission study materials are likely to do.

Public schools offer a further source of help. Among the school personnel are sure to be individuals whose training, travel, musical skills, or other abilities can be put to use. The music of other cultures and lands may be a particular resource they can supply. The school may also have useful audio-visual materials.

OUR DENOMINATIONS HELP

Our denominations make deliberate plans to strengthen the missionary education program of the local churches. The first place to inquire about these plans is at the regional headquarters—diocesan, synod, state, or conference office, however it is called. Someone there can answer questions, suggest sources of further information, and perhaps even supply what is needed. From this source are administered many schools and institutes that provide training for local leaders of education for mission. This contact with regional headquarters should be vital and regular.

The regional offices will make known what facilities the denominational headquarters is prepared to provide directly to each local church. There is the problem of missionary deputation, which we discussed earlier. Local leaders should make an effort to secure missionaries or nationals as often as possible, without expecting more than their share of such service.

Mission boards prepare informative brochures on the mission of the church; these should be distributed carefully. Good stewardship requires that printed materials reach the reader for whom they have been prepared. Dust-covered packages of pamphlets, lying unopened and completely forgotten in a dark corner of a church cabinet, are a shameful waste.

A denomination serves its members through its publications, among which the general church periodical is recommended to every home. Its pages contain many things directly or marginally related to missions. They may be clipped for future use, called to the notice of church members by public announcement, or made the subject of discussion in study groups. Certain periodicals deal specifically with the missionary enterprise. Their distribution should be greatly increased. Their columns are frequently devoted to the very study theme the local church is discussing. They are an important resource.

To complete the picture, we need to refer again to the curriculum and program publications of the denomination. The educational materials of the denomination include education about the Christian mission. Every leader in education for mission should be familiar with the mission content of these publications so that he may exploit their values when they are in use and return to them later as supplementary resources for specific study programs.

INTERDENOMINATIONAL ASSISTANCE

In the area of Christian missions, there is a great deal of interdenominational co-operation. As a result, many resources spring from interdenominational agencies. Consider first the part of the Christian mission that we customarily call home or national missions. In the National Council of the Churches of Christ, there is a Division of Home Missions through which the denominations work together to bring the redeeming power of the gospel into all areas of national life. The churches of Canada, through the Canadian Council of Churches, are increasingly working together on home missions problems.

A number of co-operative projects deserve attention in our mission study programs. There is, for example, a Christian ministry among migrant laborers in the United States under the Division of Home Missions of the National Council. This migrant ministry has area offices and field workers. During some part of each year there are migrant camps in or on the outskirts of many North American communities. Information can be secured about this work; the informed interest and participation of local churches is strongly desired. Councils of churches and councils of church women are often instrumental in organizing the migrant ministry in their localities.

There is also a Christian ministry among Indian Americans. Reservations are not nearly so generally widespread throughout the country as migrant camps, but there are Indian residents in many communities, especially in some of the large cities. The Division of Home Missions can provide information about this work as well as about another specialized ministry among Spanish Americans, who are a growing segment of our population in many places.

Interdenominational home missions activity includes co-operative planning, by which the churches hope to meet the challenges of a complex modern, urbanized society more effectively. State, provincial, and city councils of churches are intimately involved in this work, which is highly important in confronting all of the nation with the gospel of Christ.

The Division of Foreign Missions of the National Council of Churches and The Department of Overseas Mission of the Canadian Council of Churches assist denominations in co-operative missionary activity in the various geographical areas of the world and in specialized mission activities. The work is divided generally into Far East, Southeast Asia, Southern Asia, Middle East, Africa, and Latin America. Both interdenominational and denominational mission agencies are helpful sources of information.

For specialized functional ministries there are interdenominational services concerned with literacy and literature, agricultural missions, medical work, higher education, radio broadcasting, and missions to persons suffering from leprosy. An extensive program on behalf of the churches is conducted by Church World Service in the field of relief and refugee resettlement. Essential information about these activities may be secured directly or through denominational offices.

Other co-operative activities have a close relationship with the home or foreign missionary enterprise. Work in racial and cultural relations is an obvious one. Programs in international affairs, religious liberty, and pastoral counseling are similarly relevant. In each of these areas, resources of published materials and services are obtainable through denominations or the National Council of Churches.

The United Christian Youth Movement provides rich resources for work with young people. This interdenominational activity expresses itself through state, provincial, and local groups, and in denominational youth programs. Its materials and activities in the areas of Christian witness and Christian outreach are particularly useful in education for mission.

Through Youth Week themes and special emphases of study and action, co-operative youth work frequently opens a wide door of opportunity. Participation in the world mission through World Youth Projects, ecumenical institutes, and work camps make the UCYM a source of unusually exciting information and opportunity.

Among students, co-operative activity takes place through the National Student Christian Federation, an important part of which is its Commission on World Mission, the successor of the famed Student Volunteer Movement. From this source can be secured material on missionary vocations and service opportunities, and study materials for campus and church student groups.

An interdenominational resource for information about audio-visual materials is the Audio-Visual Resource Guide. In this publication, available from denominational bookstores, thousands of films and filmstrips are carefully annotated and evaluated. The listing indicates where they can be secured and how they may be used to best advantage.

THE COMMISSION ON MISSIONARY EDUCATION—FRIENDSHIP PRESS

The interdenominational agency most directly responsible for education for mission is the Commission on Missionary Education of the National Council. It is an agency of denominational boards of home missions, foreign missions, and Christian education through which missionary education materials are co-operatively prepared and published. Denominations in Canada co-operate fully as members of this commission even though it is organizationally a part of the National Council in the United States. The Committee on Missionary Education of the Canadian Council of Churches sustains a co-operative relationship with the commission. The commission's publications and productions bear the imprint, Friendship Press, Inc., a name that has become widely known as synonymous with educational materials on the Christian mission.

This co-operative enterprise has been in existence since 1902 and the name *Friendship Press* has been known in church and publishing circles since 1922. Its purpose is to extend knowledge of and commitment to the Christian mission in the whole world.

A large portion of CME's co-operative ministry is performed in the publishing of graded materials on annual study themes. These themes are selected and adopted by more than a score of denominations and made a part of the educational programs recommended to their local churches. Usually one theme on a foreign missions subject and another on a home missions topic have been chosen for each year as can be seen from the following examples:

1957-58	Japan
	Christ, the Church, and Race
1958-59	The Middle East
	Christian Concerns of North American Neighbors
1959-60	Africa
	The Church's Mission in Town and Country
1960-61	Into All the World Together
	Heritage and Horizons in Home Missions
1961-62	The Christian Mission in Latin American Countries
	Churches for New Times
1962-63	The Christian Mission on the Rim of East Asia
	The Church's Mission and Persons of Special Need
1963-64	The Christian Mission in Southern Asia
	The Changing City Challenges the Church
1964-65	The Christian Mission Among New Nations
	Spanish Americans

In addition to publications prepared especially for these annual study themes, Friendship Press publishes general resource materials. There are biographies of missionaries and Christian leaders and treatises on the theology and strategy underlying the missionary enterprise. Pictures, maps, filmstrips, plays, and pictorial booklets are provided. For leaders, an array of manuals, stories to tell, project resources, and guidance materials are provided. The basic manuals for leaders of children and youth, referred to previously, are: *Friends With All the World,* by Welker, *Wide As the World,* by Griffiths, and *In One Spirit,* by Wyckoff.

All these interdenominationally-produced materials are annotated in *Friendship Press: Complete List of Publications.* The new publications and related materials on annual study themes are described in an *Annual Announcement.* These free pamphlets, along with other descriptive leaflets and fliers, are available on request from Friendship Press or from denominational headquarters.

AND MANY OTHER SOURCES

The catalogue of possible supplementary resources for missionary education is almost endless. The daily press is an obvious one. Mission leaders know the world situation so intimately that study themes, chosen four or five years in advance, have dealt with areas of emerging crises and therefore with subjects of almost daily interest in the newspapers. An Africa study coincided with the constant news reports about the movement of many African nations toward independence. The Suez Crisis in 1958 occurred during the Middle East study. Hawaii and Alaska were admitted to statehood in the United States of America, and Cuba was in the midst of civil unrest when "Christian Concerns of North American Neighbors" was the theme. "Christ, the Church, and Race" was the missionary concern shortly after the Supreme Court decision against segregation in public education, when many cities and states were working out the application of the legal decision in their local situations. These examples illustrate how headlines and news stories provide up-to-the-minute evidence of issues raised in the mission studies.

Magazines that report or analyze the news add interpretation beyond what the daily papers present. Some specialize in current literature or sociological developments. Some, like *Holiday* or *National Geographic Magazine*, deal more with geography, culture, and places of interest. Others have a specific theological or ecclesiastical orientation and supply occasional interpretations of missionary responsibility. The offering is limitless.

Radio and television have been increasing their contributions to an understanding of our world, its people and their problems. On a few notable occasions these media reported and interpreted the Christian mission in some place or aspect of its outreach. Such programs are occasions when church groups can come together to view and discuss the presentation. More frequently, perhaps, they will be reported to a group by those who have been able to see the broadcast.

Mention should be made again of colleges and universities. Their faculties and student bodies have persons of richly varied backgrounds and competencies. An alert missionary education leader will know who may be available or how to learn about these nearby resources.

The United Nations services offer certain advantages. Information is available about the member nations. So also is descriptive material on the international service programs such as the World Health Organization, Food and Agricultural Organization, United Nations Educational, Scientific and Cultural Organization, and the work of the Trusteeship Council.

Many nations maintain information centers in large cities. These make available packets of material on their nation, describing its people, its products, and its tourist attractions.

So the list might go on. Perhaps this is enough to make clear that resources are not lacking. Cultivated, creative imagination in finding and using them is the heart of the matter.

II

Measuring Achievement

"ANYTHING THAT EXISTS, EXISTS IN SOME quantity and hence is susceptible to measurement." We can boast, for instance, of an increase in a child's height by pointing out the new mark on the kitchen doorframe. We can watch the effectiveness of a diet with the help of the bathroom scales. A church statistician can tell us whether the congregation is increasing in size or declining; he sees at a glance whether the building fund budget is in balance or askew.

But how do we gauge spiritual growth? When we are urged to "grow in the grace and knowledge of our Lord and Savior Jesus Christ" (II Pet. 3:18), how can we test our progress? If ". . . we are to grow up in every way into him who is the head, into Christ" (Eph. 4:15), by what tests can we judge the state of our health? If education for mission proposes to cultivate in children, youth, and adults understanding of and participation in the Christian world mission, must we only hope we have achieved some part of our goal?

Perhaps, as in all spiritual matters, hope and faith are the essential words. Christian attitudes and virtues can be demonstrated, but they cannot be weighed on an apothecary's balance or analyzed in the chemist's test tube. After we have done our best, we trust God's Holy Spirit to complete the work in our lives and in the lives of our friends.

Yet with a little imagination, we can find some clues that indicate what spiritual growth has occurred. Basically there are two areas in which we can take soundings. One is the program in the local church. The other is the individual church member, his attitudes and his knowledge. About the program we can ask: What has our church's missionary education program included? How adequate has it been? What has been the response of the congregation to it? Of Christian persons we must seek to discover: What is the evidence that attitudes have been changed and knowledge enlarged? In what areas is there need for further experience?

TESTING THE LOCAL CHURCH PROGRAM

A committee or an individual, concerned for the adequacy of a local church program of education for mission, might use a check list like the following to assess the merits of the program of missionary education that is being planned for the coming year:

_____ Have we discussed the mission study emphases with our pastor?

_____ Have we checked the year's church school curriculum for missionary education opportunities in it?

_____ Have we provided resources for the church school teachers to help them with their missionary education opportunities?

_____ Have we planned for a school of missions or a series of church family nights on one or both of the mission study themes of the year?

_____ Have we selected our leaders well in advance of their assignments and given them opportunities for orientation and development?

_____ Have we arranged to secure the study materials on the annual themes for our church library or leaders' bookshelf?

_____ Have we planned an exhibit or display to attract the attention and interest of the whole congregation?

_____ Have we considered how to follow up the study experiences with practical action?

This same check list will serve equally well at the close of a program year to help leaders evaluate what has happened and why.

A session of evaluation at the end of the year or at the conclusion of a particular phase of the program is always advisable. Face the facts. Was it good or was it bad? Did it succeed or did it fail? The committee or leaders might first express and discuss their own reactions. These should then be checked against the responses of the participants. In the end, without embarrassing anyone or pointing finger of blame, there should be an honest facing of failures and an accumulation of ideas that will assure a still better experience next time.

Evaluation should not be done only by the committee or individual responsible for the planning. Feed-back, a chance for members of the group to talk back to their leaders, is a creative and indispensable principle in all group activity. What did *the people* think? How do they react to what has been done?

One technique is to appoint observers who, while they participate in a program, also keep an eye on the process and the outcome. It usually works best if the other members of the group are not aware of the role these persons are playing. Their observation can then take place in a relaxed, natural way. They will watch for answers to questions like these: Did all the members of the group feel free to participate? Did the group activity maintain the interest of all? Were the real questions of the participants being asked and answered? Did learning and growth take place in any observable ways? Was the presentation too leader-centered?

At the close of the experience—either at the end of one session or of a series of sessions—these observers may be made known to the group and asked to share their reactions. Or they may be invited to sit with the committee in a post-session evaluation where their comments can be given more privately and perhaps with greater frankness. Persons performing this function will create a more objective, forthright atmosphere of assessment if they are not members of the original planning committee.

A questionnaire like the following would be useful in soliciting the written reactions of more of the participants:

What did you find most helpful in our program?

What did you find least helpful?

Rate the various elements of our program according to your own response to them:

	Excellent	Fair	Poor
Worship			
Presentations			
Discussions			
Audio-visual materials			
Leadership			
Fellowship			

What program suggestions do you have for the improvement of the program next time?

TESTING THE GROWTH OF PERSONS

The growth of persons in attitudes and knowledge is more difficult to ascertain. Since growth is a relative matter, we would need to know where persons are at the start of an educational experience in order to judge whether they have made progress as a result of it. To this end quizzes *before* and *after* may be used. In the voluntary setting of a church program these must not have the appearance of an inquisition, nor should they be used in any way that might embarrass or offend anyone. Nevertheless, the growth of understanding is so important that it deserves our serious attention. Properly handled, efforts at this kind of spiritual measurement are an unavoidable Christian duty.

Tests of information, attitude, or judgment like the following may be useful:

A TEST OF MISSIONARY OPINION[1]

(Go through the following statements as rapidly as you can, indicating first judgments without too much deliberation. If you feel a statement is more true than false, write *Yes* in front of it. If you feel it is more false than true, write *No* in front of it.)

_____ 1. So long as there is need and suffering in our own country, we ought to spend our time and money here rather than on other nations.

_____ 2. Given equal educational and cultural opportunities, persons of Caucasian background are no more intelligent or able than persons of color.

_____ 3. Migratory laborers in the United States and Canada possess civil and religious opportunities equal to most other citizens.

_____ 4. No other major religion in the world except Christianity has a missionary outreach.

_____ 5. The rapidly growing urban regions of the United States and Canada form their greatest home mission field.

_____ 6. A church that is interested in missions is more likely to be able to pay its own bills than a church not interested in missions.

_____ 7. The original Indian inhabitants of America have been treated as badly as minority or disadvantaged groups in many other countries.

_____ 8. The majority of people who become converts to Christianity in non-Christian lands do so to gain advantages of education or status.

[1] Adapted from: Harner, Nevin C. and Baker, David D. *Missionary Education in Your Church*. New York: Friendship Press, 1950, p. 163.

_____ 9. It would be helpful if the Christian churches in Asia, Africa, and Latin America sent some of their finest people to Canada and the United States as missionaries.

_____ 10. Christian principles are fully involved in the major culture-molding and decision-making forces in North America.

_____ 11. The United States, through its support of certain dictators in other lands, has earned the suspicion of nations seeking freedom and independence.

_____ 12. The religions native to Asia and Africa are as adequate for their adherents as Christianity would be.

_____ 13. Most missionaries today are highly trained people, carefully screened for their jobs.

_____ 14. Good people in other religions will be "saved," whether they learn of Jesus or not.

_____ 15. The Christian missionary enterprise is the chief force making for world brotherhood today.

_____ 16. Practically everybody in North America now has a church within easy distance.

_____ 17. Because of extensive social welfare movements and the rise of strong national churches in every land, missions will soon be unnecessary.

_____ 18. If there are underprivileged people in Canada or the United States their condition is chiefly their own fault, for which church people have no responsibility.

_____ 19. Boys and men are by nature less interested in missions than girls and women.

_____ 20. A person cannot be a good church member who is not interested in missions.

After a test like this has been taken, the various statements should be made the subject for group discussion. In some cases, the answer may not be a simple *Yes* or *No;*

conditions under which the answer might vary should be examined. The first top-of-the-head responses, nevertheless, may awaken people to an awareness of some of their deeply-held opinions that they may want to re-examine.

A TEST OF GENERAL MISSIONARY INFORMATION[2]

(Underline the statement in each case that best completes the sentence.)

1. The Great Commission is found in—the book of *Acts*, the closing chapter of *Matthew*, the opening section of *John*.

2. The great apostle to the Gentiles was—Paul, Peter, John.

3. The founder of modern missions was—Francis Xavier, St. Augustine, William Carey.

4. David Livingstone was—a Scot, an Irishman, an American.

5. Francis Asbury came as a missionary to America from—Germany, England, Scotland.

6. Buddhism is the predominant faith of—India, Indonesia, Thailand.

7. Islam is a religion whose adherents worship—one god, three gods, many gods.

8. The task of the Christian mission in North America is made difficult because the number of persons moving their residences each year is one out of every—five, ten, fifteen.

9. The Bible is now published in something over—100 different languages and dialects, 500, 1,000.

10. David Brainerd was missionary to—the South Sea Islands, the American Indians, Africa.

11. The greatest number of persons now moving into our large cities are—Roman Catholic, Protestant, Jewish.

[2] *Ibid.,* p. 165.

12. The population of the United States is increasing annually by about—3 million, 1 million, 10 million.

13. One task of national (home) missions has been—to start new churches, to raise money for missionary work abroad, to carry on missionary education in the home church.

14. The Great Missionary Awakening took place around—1700, 1800, 1900.

15. In the first century after the Reformation the Protestants were—very active in foreign missionary work, much interested in missions but unable to do much, not greatly interested in missions.

16. Missionary work has been hardest among—Confucianists, Muslims, Hindus.

17. The people of South America are principally—Protestants, Roman Catholics, adherents of no faith.

18. The chief obstacle to missionary work in recent years has been—shortage of trained missionaries, the rising tide of non-religious systems of thought, the inability of denominations to work together.

19. The new congregations being started each year in the United States and Canada number—1,000, 3,000, 5,000.

20. For every dollar the average church spends on itself, its contributions to benevolences are closest to—50¢, 30¢, 10¢.

(Answers: 1, 2nd; 2, 1st; 3, 3rd; 4, 1st; 5, 2nd; 6, 3rd; 7, 1st; 8, 1st; 9, 3rd; 10, 2nd; 11, 2nd; 12, 1st; 13, 1st; 14, 2nd; 15, 3rd; 16, 2nd; 17, 2nd; 18, 2nd; 19, 3rd; 20, 2nd.)

For particular geographical areas or specialized aspects of missionary responsibility, tests can be prepared that help to discover how much new information and understanding a group has acquired. Here is a sample of one suggested when India, Pakistan, and Ceylon were being studied:

1. How far back does the known history of each country go?
India _____, Pakistan _____, Ceylon _____

2. When did these countries become independent of foreign rule?
India _____, Pakistan _____, Ceylon _____

3. What form of government does each have today?
India _____
Pakistan _____
Ceylon _____

4. One of these countries is the size of West Virginia, another of Texas, Arkansas, and Louisiana, and the third of Europe, excluding Russia. Which is which?
India is the size of _____
Pakistan is the size of _____
Ceylon is the size of _____

5. What is the approximate population of each country?
India _____, Pakistan _____, Ceylon _____

6. What is the largest religious group in each country?
India _____, Pakistan _____, Ceylon _____

7. When did the first Protestant missionaries, Bartholomäus Ziegenbalg and Heinrich Plutschau, land in India?

8. When did William Carey, who began a new era for Protestant missions in India, arrive?
1620 _____, 1793 _____, 1860 _____

9. When did the first American missionaries in India arrive in Calcutta?
1646 _____, 1812 _____, 1870 _____

10. What is the approximate size of the total Christian community of each country?
India _____, Pakistan _____, Ceylon _____

[3] Adapted from: Cannon, Ross and Mary. *Youth Guide on India, Pakistan, and Ceylon.* New York: Friendship Press, 1954, p. 19.

Answers:

1. India, 2000 B.C.; Pakistan, 2000 B.C.; Ceylon, 500 B.C.
2. India, August, 1947; Pakistan, August, 1947; Ceylon, February, 1948.
3. India is an independent republic within the British Commonwealth; Pakistan is an independent republic within the British Commonwealth; Ceylon is a dominion within the British Commonwealth.
4. India is the size of Europe; Pakistan is the size of Texas, Arkansas, and Louisiana; and Ceylon is the size of West Virginia.
5. India, 400 million; Pakistan, 88 million; Ceylon, 9.6 million.
6. India, Hindu; Pakistan, Muslim; Ceylon, Buddhist.
7. 1706.
8. 1793.
9. 1812.
10. India, 6 million; Pakistan, 275 thousand; Ceylon, 100 thousand.

An important responsibility of education for mission is to increase the churchman's knowledge of the missionary outreach of his own denomination. A test like the following may be used to find out how much a group knows about its own communion's work:

A TEST ON THE MISSIONARY WORK OF ONE'S OWN DENOMINATION[4]

1. The lands, other than our own, in which our church is doing work are ――――――――――――――――――

2. In our own country some of the places at which our board of national (home) missions has work are ――――――

―――――――――――――――――――――――――

[4] Adapted from Harner and Baker, *op. cit.,* p. 167.

3. I think my own congregation gives about ————
a year for the support of missions both in this country and
elsewhere.

4. Some of our missionaries whose names I can think of
at present are ————————————————————

5. I remember that we have missionary schools at ——
————————————————————

6. I remember that we have missionary hospitals at ——
————————————————————

7. Our denomination has been doing missionary work since
about ————————————————————

8. Some of the greatest difficulties that our denomination
faces in its missionary work at present are ——————
————————————————————

9. The most interesting missionary incident I have ever
heard is about ————————————————————

10. The missionary books and magazines that I have read
during the past year include ——————————————
————————————————————

The test that follows is not about what people know but
about their judgment on important mission issues.

(Check the statement in each case that best completes the sentence, or add your own statement.)

1. The situation with regard to minority groups in the
United States or Canada can best be met by
————segregating the groups, giving each its own good
schools, churches, and public facilities.
————encouraging the free participation of all groups in public life as social equals.

[5] *Ibid.,* p. 168.

———assigning minority groups a permanent role of inferior status as servants and unskilled laborers.

2. The several denominational mission boards can best administer the missionary enterprise by

———acting entirely independently of one another.

———setting up a co-operative administrative relationship for work in such areas as Japan, the Middle East, Latin America.

———uniting organically in one church with a single administrative board.

3. The chief qualification of a present-day missionary at home or abroad is

———a deep and genuine Christian experience.

———a complete general academic training.

———a highly specialized training as doctor, teacher, evangelist, agricultural expert.

———a passion for Christian service.

———a thorough knowledge of the cultural background of the people among whom he will work.

———a willingness to work with and sometimes under the leaders of the church in the field to which he is sent.

4. Medical missions are valuable chiefly as

———a witness of the Christian love and brotherhood of those who establish the mission.

———alleviation of physical pain and suffering.

———a way of securing an opening for the verbal proclamation of the gospel.

5. In America the greatest undeveloped field for church work lies in

———"pockets" in some of our great cities.

———the open country.

———people with no settled abode—that is, migrants.

———new industrial areas.

———the Indian Americans.

———remote mountain and desert areas.

———the laboring population generally.

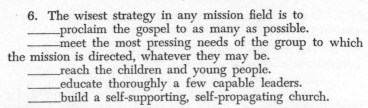

6. The wisest strategy in any mission field is to
_____proclaim the gospel to as many as possible.
_____meet the most pressing needs of the group to which the mission is directed, whatever they may be.
_____reach the children and young people.
_____educate thoroughly a few capable leaders.
_____build a self-supporting, self-propagating church.

Frequently the guidance material provided for leaders in mission study contains additional suggestions for testing. Watch for these and prepare to use them creatively. The assumption that when something has been *given out* it has been *taken in* can be very erroneous. Double check such an assumption carefully before accepting it.

Even more valuable than the use of a ready-made test is for us to construct one of our own. In fact, the study group itself might want to create one and, in doing so, summarize for itself and fix in everyone's mind some of the more important facts learned and new insights achieved.

Test, review, remember, assimilate. These principles make the learning experience profitable.

12

The Sum of It All

THE CHRISTIAN CHURCH HAS ONE MISSION IN the world, the mission of its one Lord. That mission is to bear witness among people so that they may know God and know themselves as his children, reconciled to him through their faith in Jesus Christ.

That mission is the character and the quality of life of the whole church when the church is true to its nature and calling. The mission expresses itself vividly in the missionary thrust that carries a congregation out beyond itself to those horizons near and far where the evangelization of the world occurs. Home and foreign missions have been the faithful effort of the churches to respond to the call of God, and in our day, this effort is seen ever more clearly to be one mission to the whole world.

Each Christian congregation has the duty to nurture its members in the fulness of the Christian life, relying on the Holy Spirit to enlarge and consecrate what human hands and minds attempt. Nurture in the specific missionary obligations and opportunities confronting the church in its own generation is an imperative part of this educational task. We call this nurture education for mission.

Education for mission is at once exciting and challenging. It has to do with the timely and critical issues that the Christian cause is facing in a changing world. It deserves careful planning, skillful execution, and adequate opportunity.

Leaders are the key to success in education for mission. The interest of the minister is essential, but the task can be done only if laymen and minister work together. The dedication and enthusiasm of the leaders will make them ready instruments for the task. A wealth of resources is at their hand. Discipline and training will increase their skill and season them for the duty.

Their field is the whole church—children, youth, women, men. Here is no specialty for the Christian with time to spare or with a penchant for missions. This call to growth in mission is for every Christian so he may move constantly toward ". . . the measure of the stature of the fulness of Christ. . . ." (Eph. 4:13.)

Many of us may be new in leadership in education for mission. This book is intended to guide such newcomers to an effective and joyful meeting of their responsibilities. Others of us are already skilled and experienced; the reading of these pages may have helped us renew our understanding of the task and led us to new visions of achievement.

All of us are called to strive for a growing involvement of all the people of the church in the Christian mission. It is Christ's mission in the world to which the church is called. As we respond in faith, there is the promise that we have: ". . . lo, I am with you always, to the close of the age." (Matt. 28:20.)

Reading List

MISSION

Anderson, Gerald H. *The Theology of the Christian Mission.* New York: McGraw-Hill Book Co. Inc., 1961.

Bavinck, J. H. *An Introduction to the Science of Missions.* Philadelphia: Presbyterian & Reformed Pub. Co., 1960.

Douglass, Truman B. *Mission to America.* New York: Friendship Press, 1951.

Goodall, Norman (ed.). *Missions Under the Cross; Addresses . . . [International Missionary Council meeting] at Willingen . . .* New York: Friendship Press, 1953.

Handy, Robert T. *We Witness Together.* New York: Friendship Press, 1957.

Hoffman, James. *Mission U.S.A.* New York: Friendship Press, 1956.

Hogg, W. Richey. *One World, One Mission.* New York: Friendship Press, 1960.

Kraemer, Hendrik. *The Christian Message in a Non-Christian World.* New York: Harper & Brothers, 1938. (Rev. ed., London, Eng.: James Clarke & Co., Ltd., 1957.)

Kraemer, Hendrik. *Religion and the Christian Faith.* Philadelphia: Westminster Press, 1957.

Levai, Blaise. *Revolution in Missions.* Calcutta, India: YMCA Publishing House (distributed by Friendship Press), 1957.

The Life and Mission of the Church; A Study Outline. Geneva, Switz.: World's Student Christian Federation, 1959.

McGavran, Donald A. *The Bridges of God*. New York: Friendship Press, 1955.

McGavran, Donald A. *How Churches Grow*. London, Eng.: World Dominion Press (distributed by Friendship Press), 1959.

Manikam, Rajah B. *Christianity and the Asian Revolution*. New York: Friendship Press, 1955.

Mathews, Basil. *Forward Through the Ages*. New York: Friendship Press, rev. ed., 1960.

The Methodist Church. Joint Section of Education and Cultivation, Board of Missions (ed.). *The Christian Mission Today*. Nashville, Tenn.: Abingdon Press, 1960.

Neill, Stephen. *The Unfinished Task*. London, Eng.: Lutterworth Press, 1957.

Newbigin, Lesslie. *One Body, One Gospel, One World; The Christian Mission Today*. London, Eng.: International Missionary Council, 1958.

Niles, D. T. *That They May Have Life*. New York: Harper & Brothers, 1951.

Pickhard, Elsie C. and Shotwell, Louisa R. *Every Tribe and Tongue*. New York: Friendship Press, 1960.

Ranson, Charles W. *That the World May Know*. New York: Friendship Press, 1953.

Spike, Robert W. *Safe in Bondage*. New York: Friendship Press, 1960.

Warren, Max A. C. *Caesar: The Beloved Enemy*. Napierville, Ill.: Alec P. Allenson, Inc. (for Student Christian Movement), 1955.

Warren, Max A. C. *The Christian Mission*. London, Eng.: Student Christian Movement Press, (distributed by Friendship Press), 1951.

EDUCATION FOR MISSION

Allstrom, Elizabeth. *Let's Play a Story*. New York: Friendship Press, 1957.

Griffiths, Louise B. *Wide As the World: Junior Highs and Missions.* New York: Friendship Press, 1958.

Keiser, Armilda B. *Here's How and When.* New York: Friendship Press, 1952.

Millen, Nina (ed.). *Missionary Stories to Play and Tell.* New York: Friendship Press, 1958.

Welker, Edith F. *Friends With All the World.* New York: Friendship Press, 1954.

Wyckoff, D. Campbell. *In One Spirit: Senior Highs and Missions.* New York: Friendship Press, 1958.

CHRISTIAN EDUCATION

Forsyth, Daird and Howard, Wilbur. *The Growing Superintendent.* Toronto, Canada: Canadian Council of Churches, 1960.

Foster, Virgil E. *How a Small Church Can Have Good Christian Education.* New York: Harper & Brothers, 1956.

Gable, Lee J. *Encyclopedia for Church Group Leaders.* New York: National Council of Churches, 1955.

Gable, Lee J. *Encyclopedia for Church Group Leaders.* New York: Association Press, 1959.

Harner, Nevin. *The Educational Work of the Church.* Nashville, Tenn.: Abingdon Press, 1939.

Kuhn, Margaret E. *You Can't Be Human Alone.* New York: National Council of Churches, 1956.

Little, Sara. *Learning Together in the Christian Fellowship.* Richmond, Va.: John Knox Press, 1956.

The Objectives of Christian Education for Senior High Young People. New York: National Council of Churches, 1958.

Owen, Edward F. Jr. *A Manual for Young Adults.* New York: National Council of Churches, 1960.

Vieth, Paul H. *The Church School; Organization, Administration and Supervision.* . . . Philadelphia: Christian Education Press, 1957.

Wyckoff, D. Campbell. *The Gospel and Christian Education.* Philadelphia: Westminster Press, 1959.

Wyckoff, D. Campbell. *The Task of Christian Education.* Philadelphia: Westminster Press, 1955.

WORKING WITH GROUPS

Blumenthal, Louis H. *How to Work With Your Board and Committees.* New York: Association Press, 1954.

Clemmons, Robert S. *Dynamics of Christian Adult Education.* Nashville, Tenn.: Abingdon Press, 1958.

Douglass, Paul F. *The Group Workshop Way in the Church.* New York: Association Press, 1956.

Douty, Mary Alice. *How to Work With Church Groups.* Nashville, Tenn.: Abingdon Press, 1957.

Frank, Lawrence. *How to be a Modern Leader.* New York: Association Press, 1954.

How to Lead Discussions. (Leadership Pamphlet, no. 1) Chicago: Adult Education Association of the U.S.A., 1955.

How to Teach Adults. (Leadership Pamphlet, no. 5.) Chicago: Adult Education Association of the U.S.A., 1955.

How to Use Role Playing. (Leadership Pamphlet, no. 6) Chicago: Adult Education Association of the U.S.A. 1955.

Kelley, Earl. *The Workshop Way of Learning.* New York: Harper & Brothers, 1951.

Klein, Alan F. *Role Playing.* New York: Association Press, 1956.

Knowles, Malcolm and Hulda. *Introduction to Group Dynamics.* New York: Association Press, 1959.

Strauss, Bert and Frances. *New Ways to Better Meetings.* New York: Viking Press, 1951.

Understanding How Groups Work. (Leadership Pamphlet, no. 4.) Chicago: Adult Education Association of the U.S.A., 1955.

WORSHIP RESOURCES

Fleming, Daniel Johnson. *Each With His Own Brush.* New York: Friendship Press, 1952.

Maus, Cynthia Pearl. *Christ and the Fine Arts.* New York: Harper & Brothers, 1938.

——————. *The Church and the Fine Arts.* New York: Harper & Brothers, 1960.

Thomas, Edith Lovell (comp.). *The Whole World Singing.* New York: Friendship Press, 1950.

ABOUT THE FORMAT

This book was set in Linotype Caledonia 10 point
leaded 3 points. Designed by the late W. A. Dwig-
gins, this face belongs to the "modern" family of type
faces and is somewhat similar to Scotch Modern, although more freely drawn than that letter.

Manufactured by Sowers Printing Company, Lebanon, Pa.
Jackets and covers by Affiliated Lithographers, Inc.,
New York, N. Y.
Paper: S. D. Warren's #66 Antique
Typographic design by Margery W. Smith
Binding by Louise E. Jefferson